The Cathedral of the World

AS AUTHOR

Father and Son: A Personal Biography of Senator Frank Church of Idaho

The Devil & Dr. Church: A Guide to Hell for Atheists and True Believers

Entertaining Angels: A Guide to Heaven for Atheists and True Believers

The Seven Deadly Virtues: A Guide to Purgatory for Atheists and True Believers

Everyday Miracles: Stories from Life

A Chosen Faith: An Introduction to Unitarian Universalism
(with John A. Buehrens)

*God and Other Famous Liberals:
Recapturing Bible, Flag, and Family from the Far Right*

Life Lines: Holding On (and Letting Go)

Lifecraft: The Art of Meaning in the Everyday

The American Creed: A Biography of the Declaration of Independence

Bringing God Home: A Spiritual Guidebook for the Journey of Your Life

Freedom from Fear: Finding the Courage to Love, Act, and Be

*So Help Me God: The Founding Fathers and
the First Great Battle over Church and State*

Love & Death: My Journey through the Valley of the Shadow

AS EDITOR

Continuities and Discontinuities in Church History (with Timothy George)

The Essential Tillich

The Macmillan Book of Earliest Christian Prayers (with Terrence J. Mulry)

The Macmillan Book of Earliest Christian Hymns (with Terrence J. Mulry)

The Macmillan Book of Earliest Christian Meditations
(with Terrence J. Mulry)

One Prayer at a Time (with Terrence J. Mulry)

Without Apology: Collected Meditations on Liberal Religion
(by A. Powell Davies)

The Jefferson Bible

Restoring Faith: America's Religious Leaders Answer Terror with Hope

*The Separation of Church and State:
Writings on a Fundamental Freedom by America's Founders*

The Cathedral of the World

A Universalist Theology

FORREST CHURCH

Beacon Press
Boston

Beacon Press
25 Beacon Street
Boston, Massachusetts 02108-2892
www.beacon.org

Beacon Press books
are published under the auspices of
the Unitarian Universalist Association of Congregations.

13   12   11   10   8   7   6   5   4   3   2   1

This book is printed on acid-free paper that meets the uncoated paper
ANSI/NISO specifications for permanence as revised in 1992.

Text design by Yvonne Tsang
at Wilsted & Taylor Publishing Services, Oakland, CA

Library of Congress Cataloging-in-Publication Data

Church, F. Forrester.
The cathedral of the world : a universalist theology / Forrest Church.
        p. cm.
ISBN 978-0-8070-0621-4 (paperback : alk. paper) 1. Liberalism (Religion)
    2. Unitarian Universalist churches—Doctrines. I. Title.
                    BR1615.C475 2009
230'.9132—dc22   2009018751

To Carolyn, the love of my life

Contents

Introduction

In February 2008 I received my death sentence. The warning bell had rung a year and a half before. After living in cancer's shadow for a surprisingly uneventful span following the November 2006 removal of my esophagus (together, we hoped, with the disease that had riddled it), my luck ran out. The cancer had returned with a vengeance. Stage IV esophageal cancer, the medical terrain I now occupy, is incurable. Not without reason (though supplementing my doctor's cautious reckoning with imprudent visits to the Internet), slightly more than a year ago I was measuring the life remaining to me, if not in coffee spoons, certainly not in years.

With time now on the march, I determined to write one final book, *Love & Death: My Journey through the Valley of the Shadow*. Returning to Beacon Press, where publisher Helene Atwan graciously welcomed me back into the fold, I dispatched the book swiftly, for both practical and spiritual reasons—notably to avoid getting caught facing two deadlines at once. Beacon rushed the book, beautifully produced, into print by June, an act of robust skill and true kindness for which I shall always be grateful.

Admittedly, I wrote *Love & Death* in a slightly enhanced state. Not yet accustomed to the steroids my oncologist was doling out to help me tolerate an intensive weekly chemotherapy regimen, I could easily go forty hours a stretch without sleeping. As I told my congregation, I hadn't been so high since the late '60s.

For a time, my journey toward death sailed along as anticipated. By May, I had lost twenty-five pounds. Death hovered closer every day, or certainly seemed to. But then the tables turned. I gained all my weight back and began feeling better physically. Meanwhile, the tumors, scattered throughout my lungs and liver, dwindled to almost nothing, offering a year's reprieve. As the poison did its work, I lived in a kind of suspended animation. My death interrupted, life became timeless. Near the end of this welcome hiatus, a year dedicated in part to reading hundreds of books—it's like dying and going to heaven— I got the itch to write another one myself.

Under the canopy of my ministerial calling, I've been blessed with three distinct vocations: as a pastor first and foremost, but also as a historian and liberal theologian. In early 2007, during recovery from my cancer operation, I finished the sprawling narrative history I'd always hoped to write, *So Help Me God: The Founding Fathers and the First Great Battle over Church and State*. This accomplishment rounded off my historical trajectory, launched more than thirty years earlier when I received my doctoral degree in church history.

In 2008 *Love & Death* put a capstone on my pastoral career, summing up what I had learned during my three-decade tenure as senior minister of All Souls Unitarian Church in Manhattan. I loved writing that book. It offered me a final pastoral opportunity. And it gave me the chance to ponder life and death from a new, more intimate, perspective. There was only one problem. When my renewed lease on life made it possible for me to consider writing one more "final" book, *Love & Death* didn't naturally lend itself to a sequel.

Only one genre of my work remained incomplete. I had not systematically laid out my universalist theology. I'd never gathered my thoughts on religion, faith, and God in a single volume. So I decided to seize this unanticipated gift of time to frame my theological teachings. Drawn in equal thirds from new material, previously uncollected articles and addresses, and selections from my earlier books (all thoroughly revised and reimagined), *The Cathedral of the World* completes the arc of my third vocation—as a universalist theologian.

Universalism speaks with particular eloquence to the challenge of our times. Today our neighbors live not only across the street, but across the world as well. During an age when we share a global economy and communications system in addition to nuclear and environmental threats, universalism addresses our era's most dangerous dysfunction: theological parochialism. Every denomination, including my own Unitarian Universalist Association, can fall prey to such nearsightedness. To fulfill its promise, modern universalism must witness against fundamentalists on the left as well as those on the right. By definition, "universalism" is not the property of any discrete religious body, including those that include it in their names.

To illustrate this point, which pivots at the center of my theology, let me take you on a brief initial journey. We shall walk together to the water's edge and follow the light of the moon wherever it may lead.

We are standing on the shoreline of a mountain lake, moonlight lapping against our boot tips, mesmerized by the golden carpet laid out over the water as if lowered from the heavens to meet us at the very place we stand. Before us, along the moon's glorious trail, we can see all the way to the lake's rocky bottom. Above the sunken branches, we watch the water dance and sparkle, a rack of moonbeams on each ripple's crest. Across the lake, where the moon is rising, our path turns to liquid gold.

Standing on the shore some distance to our right, a man contemplates the same view yet appears shrouded in darkness. To our left stands a woman, her silhouette all but obscured by the blackness that envelops her.

Pondering these two apparently benighted people, we wonder to ourselves, "What can they possibly be thinking? Encompassed by darkness, the lake before them flat and lifeless, if only they would join us at the foot of the moon's luminous path, they, too, could bathe in celestial light."

Henry David Thoreau once chastised the Florentine artist and adventurer Benvenuto Cellini for mistaking the aura he saw surrounding his shadow on a dew-drenched day as a special sign of divine recognition. In the moonlight, we experience a like illusion, as do the man and woman to our right and left, who share our vision though we perceive them to be in darkness. Judging only by what they see, they, too, may feel themselves uniquely illumined. To their eyes, it is we who appear to languish in darkness.

Expressive of both the wonder and danger of religion, on the one hand, the moon's golden light extends a path across the lake to the feet of everyone who stands under the spell of its supernal glow; on the other, given that each onlooker sees only his or her own golden pathway, all others standing in apparent darkness, we are left with the impression that we walk the one true path alone, whereas those who fail to join us are lost. Here nature can serve as our theological tutor. She reminds us that, in almost every way that matters, we and our most distant neighbor, sprung from a single source and sharing the same destiny, are one. This revelation encapsulates the essence of universalist theology. To perceive things as they are, not merely as they appear, we must view them with parallax vision. We must imagine seeing them through others' eyes as well as through our own.

The Cathedral of the World begins with a like metaphor ("one light and many windows") drawn from the introduction to Unitarian Universalism that I wrote with my colleague John Buehrens. Although tailor-made for my own denomination—Unitarian, "one light," Universalist, "many windows"—my cathedral metaphor weaves an all-embracing theological garment, suitable for universalists of every religious persuasion.

Since universalism springs from a set of liberal religious propositions, I follow this opening statement of universalist principles by offering evidence for a liberal interpretation of the divine. I am a born-again liberal. My religious liberalism is unapologetic—enthusiastic and unabashed. The word "liberal" means openhearted, openhanded, and open-minded. We need only consult the dictionary to reclaim this much-abused word. Liberal means free; worthy of a free person (as opposed to servile); free in bestowing, bountiful and generous; free from bigotry or unreasonable prejudice in favor of traditional opinions or teachings; open to the reception of new ideas. The phrase "dogmatic liberal" is an oxymoron. Unlike every form of fundamentalism, the liberal religious spirit grows and moves. Revelation is not sealed.

I open with a full-throated celebration of liberalism, freely adapting two chapters from my book *God and Other Famous Liberals.* It was there that I initiated a career-long quest: to reclaim Bible, flag, and family from their late captivity by the religious right. Book I addresses the first and third of these still unfinished tasks, reclaiming Bible and family.

In Book II, "The American Creed," I tackle the second task: reclaiming America's most powerful symbols as liberal symbols, not conservative ones. Consider the United States motto, expressive of our nation at its aspirational best: *E pluribus unum,* "Out of many, one." Like my cathedral metaphor, this motto captures the spirit of universalism. Liberal religion was present at the nation's founding. In the Declaration of Independence, the United States of America threw down a challenging ethical gauntlet: liberty and justice for all. This egalitarian mandate, grounded in nature and nature's God, has strong liberal religious underpinnings and animates what I, not uniquely, call the American Creed.

Book III I dedicate to the liberal pulpit. Even as the Gospels define Jesus Christ as the word made flesh, for me a sermon is the flesh made word. No presentation of my faith would be complete without a representative selection of sermons. The pulpit is my forge, where week after week, in response to the call of the hour, I have hammered out my theology. More than a sample of opinions on issues of the day, the third section of this book captures universalism in action.

I unpack my theology in a more systematic way in Book IV. It builds toward a mature credo statement, "Universalism for the Twenty-first Century." Although I originally addressed several pieces in this section to members of the Unitarian Universalist Association, they nonetheless lay a foundation on which to build a contemporary universalist theology within almost any faith tradition. I close this exploration of universalist principles with two excerpts adapted from *Bringing God Home*, in some ways my favorite, most personal, book.

I shall leave you in Book V with some thoughts I find myself pondering in preparation for my death, postponed though it may be. The publication of *Love & Death* elicited a number of radio and television interviews, one of which I include here, together with further reflections on the subject of love (the heart of the universalist gospel) drawn from a sermon I preached in early 2009.

Finally, for my benediction, I reach back to my first book, *Father and Son: A Personal Biography of Senator Frank Church of Idaho*, written in 1984 during the summer following my father's death. Universalism emerges from the shadows as clearly as it does from the light.

Though I view the one light most receptively through my own chosen windows, *The Cathedral of the World* lays out the nonsectarian underpinnings of a twenty-first-century universalist faith. Partly in the hope that we will take our own name more seriously, I present it first to that hardy little band of freethinkers who call themselves Unitarian Universalists. They have offered me a home in which to formulate and test out my theology. For this, I remain eternally grateful. Cognizant of their potential saving impact on and in the world we share, I offer it also and with equal gratitude to universalists in other faith traditions. Given the breadth and scope of the universalist gospel, theologically we hold so much more in common than could ever divide us. Finally, I extend my hand to the unchurched seeker. You, too, are on a journey, a quest for life's meaning and purpose. I believe both can be found in universalism, where you may discover, as I have, that to be saved without damning another is a wonderful thing.

The Cathedral of the World

Imagine awakening one morning from a deep and dreamless sleep to find yourself in the nave of a vast cathedral. Like a child new-born, untutored save to moisture, nurture, rhythm, and the profound comforts at the heart of darkness, you open your eyes onto a world unseen, indeed unimaginable, before. It is a world of light and dancing shadow, stone and glass, life and death. This second birth, at once miraculous and natural, is in some ways not unlike the first. A new awakening, it consecrates your life with sacraments of pain you do not understand and promised joy you will never fully call your own.

Such awakenings may happen once in a lifetime or many times. But when they do, what before you took for granted is presented as a gift: challenging, yet precious and good. Not that you know what to do with your gift, or even what it really means, only how much it matters. Awakening to the call stirring deep within you, the call of life itself, the call of God, you begin your pilgrimage.

Before you do, look about you. Contemplate the mystery and contemplate with awe. This cathedral is as ancient as humankind, its cornerstone the first altar, marked with the tincture of blood and blessed by tears. Search for a lifetime (which is all you are surely given) and you shall never know its limits, visit all its transepts, worship at its myriad shrines, nor span its celestial ceiling with your gaze. The builders have worked from time immemorial, destroying and creating, confounding and perfecting, tearing down and raising up arches in this cathedral, buttresses and chapels, organs, theaters and chancels, gargoyles, idols, and icons. Not a moment passes without work being begun that shall not be finished in the lifetime of the architects who planned it, the patrons who paid for it, the builders who constructed it, and the expectant worshippers. Throughout human history, one generation after another has labored lovingly, sometimes fearfully, crafting memorials and consecrating shrines. Untold numbers of these collect dust in long-undisturbed chambers; others (cast centuries or eons ago from their once-respected places) lie shattered in chards or ground into powder on the cathedral floor. Not a moment passes without the dreams of long-dead dreamers being outstripped, crushed, or abandoned, giving way to new visions, each immortal in reach, ephemeral in grasp.

Welcome to the Cathedral of the World.

Above all else, contemplate the windows. In the Cathedral of the World there are windows beyond number, some long forgotten, covered with many patinas of grime, others revered by millions, the most sacred of shrines. Each in its own way is beautiful. Some are abstract, others representational; some dark and meditative, others bright and dazzling. Each window tells a story about the creation of the world, the meaning of history, the purpose of life, the nature of humankind, the mystery of death. The windows of the cathedral are where the light shines through.

Because the cathedral is so vast, our life so short, and our vision so dim, over the course of our pilgrimage we are able to contemplate only a bit of the cathedral, explore a few apses, reflect on the play of light and darkness through a few of its myriad windows. Yet, by pondering and acting on our ruminations, we discover insights that will invest our days with meaning.

A twenty-first-century theology based on the concept of one light and many windows offers to its adherents both breadth and focus. Honoring multiple religious approaches, it only excludes the truth-claims of absolutists. That is because fundamentalists claim that the light shines through their window only. Some, as we know from painful recent experience, go so far as to beseech their followers to throw stones through other people's windows.

Skeptics draw the opposite conclusion. Seeing the bewildering variety of windows and observing the folly of the worshippers, they conclude that there is no light. But the windows are not the light. They are where the light shines through.

We shall never see the light directly, only as refracted through the windows of the cathedral. Prompting humility, life's mystery lies hidden. The light is veiled. Yet, being halfway in size between the creation itself and our body's smallest constituent part, that we can encompass with our minds the universe that encompasses us is a cause for great wonder. Awakened by the light, we stand in the cathedral, trembling with awe.

Some people have trouble believing in a God who looks into any eyes but theirs. Others have trouble believing in a God they cannot see. But that none of us can look directly into God's eyes certainly doesn't mean God isn't there, mysterious, unknowable, gazing into ours through the windows of the Cathedral of the World.

BOOK I

God and Other Famous Liberals

CHAPTER I

The Greatest Liberal of Them All

Beginning in the mid-1970s, Christian fundamentalists, in groups such as Jerry Falwell's Moral Majority and Pat Robertson's Christian Coalition, began to organize politically, following a tack they had rejected during the civil rights movement, when they argued that religion and politics should never mix. Reversing field, they were now preaching politics with a vengeance. Liberals and liberal policies were unbiblical, un-American, and antifamily, they claimed. These claims drove many liberal religionists into a reactive posture. We dismissed the Bible's validity in the public square (something Martin Luther King Jr. would never have done), wore American flag pins upside down on our lapels (condescendingly describing this as a nautical distress signal), and were more vocal in our defense of pornography as a form of free speech than we were quick to defend our own deeply felt family values. Even some of the terms appropriated by the right, "pro-life" being the most prominent example, carried more weight than their opposite numbers, in this case "pro-choice." To me, the irony was that liberal-minded people were aligned more closely than were those on the religious right to the spirit of the Bible, the principles set forth by our country's founders, and the needs of America's families. In my book God and Other Famous Liberals, I sought to reclaim the potent symbols of Bible, flag, and family to advance the liberal cause.

Who is the most famous liberal of all time? It simply has to be God. No one is more generous, bounteous, or misunderstood. Not to mention profligate. Take a look at the creation. God is a lavish and indiscriminate host. There is too much of everything: creatures, cultures, languages, stars; more galaxies than we can count; more asteroids in the heavens than grains of sand on earth. Talk about self-indulgence. In the ark itself, if you take the story literally, there must have been (by scientific reckoning) a million pairs of insects. We may not like it, but that's the way it is.

Every word I can conjure for God is a synonym for liberal. God is munificent and openhanded. The creation is exuberant, lavish, even prodigal. As the ground of our being, God is ample and plenteous. As healer and comforter, God is charitable and benevolent. As our redeemer, God is generous and forgiving. And God has a bleeding heart that simply never stops. Liberal images such as these spring from every page of creation's text. They also characterize the spirit, if not always the letter, of the Bible, which teaches us that God is love.

Admittedly, God's love is hard to approximate. To begin with, God created us in different colors; we come in many faiths, with varying sexual preferences, a whole spectrum of political views, and widely disparate tastes in culture and dress. Such variety raises the level of difficulty as we try to live together in amity. It also requires that, created in God's image, we cultivate the liberal spirit, especially as it enjoins open-mindedness and respect for those who differ from us, each a necessary virtue in our pluralistic world.

Though experience and observation lead me to describe God as a liberal, "liberal" is not a big enough word for God. God is more than liberal, much more generous and neighborly, far more imprudent than the wildest liberal on your block. Most revealing of all, God's gift to us is beyond anything we deserve or could possibly have expected: the gift of life.

In the early Middle Ages, one school of mystical theologians, Dionysius the Areopagite principal among them, argued that, given the limitations of our knowledge and vocabulary, the best way to describe God is by saying what God is not. Following Dionysius we can turn things around and say with great confidence that God is not illiberal. God is not miserly, parsimonious, penurious, or stingy. God is not narrow or rigid. Neither closefisted nor tightfisted, God is never spare when giving change.

God language can tie people into knots, of course. In part, that is because "God" is not God's name. Referring to the highest power we can imagine, "God" is our name for that which is greater than all and yet present in each. For some the highest imaginable power will be a petty and angry tribal baron ensconced high above the clouds on a golden throne, visiting punishment on all who don't believe in him. But for others, the highest power is love, goodness, justice, or the spirit of life itself. Each of us projects our limited experience on a cosmic screen in letters as big as our minds can fashion. For those whose vision is constricted (illiberal, narrow-minded people), this can have horrific consequences. But others respond to the munificence of creation with broad imagination and sympathy. Answering to the highest and best within and beyond themselves, they draw lessons and fathom meaning so redemptive that surely it touches the divine.

Proposing that "God" is not God's name is anything but blasphemous. When Moses asks whom he is talking to up there on Mount Sinai, the answer is not "God," but "I am who I am," or "I do what I do." That's what the word "Yahweh" means. When the Hebrews later insisted that it not be written out in full, they were guarding against idolatry: the worshipping of a part (in this case the word-symbol for God) in place of the whole (that toward which the word-symbol points).

So it was for the biblical Jacob, who wrestled for life and meaning with a mysterious heavenly messenger. When dawn finally broke after the nightlong struggle, Jacob demanded to know his adversary's name. "Don't worry about my name," God replied. "It is completely unimportant. All that matters is that you held your own during a night of intense struggle. You will walk with a limp for the remainder of your days. Yet that is simply proof that in wrestling for meaning you did not retreat, but gave your all. Therefore, though my name is unimportant, I shall give you a new name, Israel, 'one who wrestled with both divinity and humanity, and prevailed.'"

Politicians and theologians who trumpet "God is on our side" often forget what Jacob learned through his night of struggle: humility is a virtue. At least Jacob, in learning his limits, proved himself worthy of God's blessing. When we kill or hate in God's name, we blaspheme creator and creation alike.

Simply turn on the evening news. Somewhere on our shrinking planet, terrorists for truth and God are blowing up airplanes and cars, embassies and hotels. All across the world God's self-proclaimed champions fight to the death, raising a gun in one hand and a Bible, the Koran, or some other holy book in the other. Many of our ancestors did the same, equipped with proof texts to drive home the point of their spears. Far too often war is synonymous with religious war: Catholic against Protestant; Shiite against Sunni; Muslim against Christian, Jew, or Hindu. Even the Greek gods chose sides.

Religious passion is human passion writ large. Throughout history millions of people have killed or died in God's name. There are reasons for this. When we care deeply, it is because we believe fiercely. That is especially true of religious belief. Our very salvation is at stake. In contests with underlying religious motivation, it seems that we and our enemy cannot both be right. Too often what escapes us is that we both may be wrong.

Religious wars of words can be equally ferocious. Spiritual leaders have long since perfected the rhetoric of bellicosity to damn their chosen adversaries. Even those right-wing Christians, Islamic warriors, and Jewish fundamentalists who don't go in for explosives often enlist as soldiers for a vengeful God who damns more often than he saves, a hanging judge serving their own narrow interests or creed. When such individuals assign the name "God" to the highest power they can imagine, their experience may construe this power to be as brutal as a wicked stepparent, imperious as an absolute monarch, strict as a boot-camp sergeant, and wanton as an invading marauder.

It is impossible for me to believe in such a God. Projecting my limited experience of the greatest concepts I know—love, goodness, generosity, kindness, compassion, and neighborliness—I see not a monarch (powerful, distant, judgmental, capricious, and controlling) but the spirit of love, working with us not against us, in a cooperative relationship, and for our common good. Reading both the tea

4

leaves of creation and the high points of scripture, I can think of few adjectives that encompass the sweep, vitality, and heart implicit in the creation and capture the Bible more eloquently than does the word "liberal."

People sometimes tell me they don't believe in God. "Tell me a little about the God you don't believe in," I reply. "I probably don't believe in him either." I certainly don't believe in the great father in the sky armed with a bolt of lightning aimed at the heart of his adversaries. I don't believe in a God who saves some people from airplane crashes, earthquakes, or hurricanes, while grinding others to dust under his merciless heel. I don't believe in a God who glibly chooses sides, and then brings in the heavy artillery, not to mention a God who helps one team trounce the other in the Super Bowl. If the God they disbelieve in is anything like the God I disbelieve in, their God is too small.

Religion should never be small. Religion is our human response to the dual reality of being alive and knowing we must die. We humans are not the animal with tools or the animal with advanced language. We are the religious animal. On discovering that we must die, we question what life means. Who are we? Where did we come from? Where are we going and why? These are religious questions. Children ask them. So do adults, when we can't avoid them. When a loved one dies, or we are given three months to live, the roof caves in on our carefully circumscribed existence. But we also ask these same questions when life, in all its awe-inspiring majesty, dazzles us and blows the roof away.

Being human and therefore limited, we cannot define God's nature, not finally, but for many Jews and Christians, the Bible helps. Created in God's image, we are called on to manifest the same spirit of love, generosity, and selflessness that inspired the patriarchs, prophets, and Jesus, whose stories fill the Bible's most telling pages. Judging from the spirit of the scriptures, wonderfully captured in legend and parable, God is not merely a liberal, but a liberal with a capital *L*.

Given our penchant for literalism, to understand how and why these stories work, think of your own grandparents. For many of us, the stories we tell about them are a mixture of fact and truth, the lat-

5

ter an exaggerated or legendary version of the former. Stories drawn from their lives contain lessons that are clearer than the details themselves might suggest. From our grandparents' stories, we winnow lessons to help us become better people. They did the same, inspired by their grandparents' stories. Sometimes the facts get lost, yet truth is served.

I could tell you how my maternal grandfather, Chase Clark, lost his bid for reelection as governor because he let two hundred nonviolent prisoners free from the Idaho penitentiary, which in 1942 was rife with overcrowding; or how he sacrificed everything to move to Salt Lake City for six months when my grandmother was pregnant with my mother, to ensure that she (having lost her first child) would have good hospital care; or how, as a young Idaho lawyer, he bought new shoes for his clients, so that they wouldn't catch cold in jail. Each of these stories is based on fact, but their truth over years of retelling has more to do with a combination of selective detail and distillation, which together make them memorable and moving.

If true of the stories we tell about people we know, what does this suggest about stories passed down from generation to generation, stories of distant ancestors, the heroes of our nation or our faith? They, too, are purified over time, unencumbered of incidental fact, focused for impact, and distilled into truth.

Skeptics dispute this. They argue that the varnish must be stripped away for us to see the cold, hard facts and be undeceived concerning our ancestors' and forebears' questionable nobility. I don't completely disagree. It makes me feel a little less inadequate to know that my parents found a bottle of whiskey in my teetotaling grandfather's desk after he died. But I still pass on other stories of his life to my children, stories that over time have begun to develop legendary features. I do this because such stories inspire both my children and me to be better people and to lead more loving lives.

The same is true of the Bible. It, too, is a kind of family history, a treasure trove of stories passed down from generation to generation, distilled, revised, and improved over centuries until the stories finally were fixed into scripture. In presenting God's word and inviting us to divine and then imitate God's will, the biblical authors drew analogies from human experience that suggested the nature of divine reality.

The story of Abraham and Sarah, for instance, attests directly to the holy spirit, by providing a liberal mandate always to be generous and neighborly, especially to strangers. When Abraham and Sarah provided hospitality to three strangers, they opened their door, shared what little bread they had, and offered shelter from the elements. As promised (the three strangers being angels in disguise), despite Sarah's doubts and against all logic, this old man and his old wife subsequently parented a child, Isaac, the seed of Israel.

Interpreting this story, fundamentalists of the right insist that Sarah had a child when she was one hundred years old. Fundamentalists of the left cite the scriptures of science to offer conclusive proof that this is laughable, impossible, an insult to the intelligence in defiance of nature's laws. Both miss the point. As many good people from the biblical era until now have understood, the lesson spoken here—"Be kind to strangers"—has little to do with either fact or dogma. The story is about opening our hearts and homes to the other, the stranger and the homeless. It doesn't say, "Be kind to strangers because they may in fact be angels who give babies away as presents." It says, "Be kind to strangers because that is the right thing to do." The story of Abraham and Sarah, great-great-grandparents of Muslim, Jew, and Christian alike, inspires us to be more generous people. Is this story factual? Almost certainly not. Is it true? Absolutely, for it leads us to honor others by being true to the best in ourselves.

This ethical impulse drives liberal religion. It also taps into the marrow of the Bible. Jesus rejected the pieties of the local religious establishment. He followed a higher law, the law of God, which was expressed by the spirit of the scriptures rather than in their letter. The earliest followers of Jesus responded to the biblical literalists of their own day in like manner. The spirit of the scriptures gives life, Saint Paul said; the letter kills. And the apostle James pointed out that faith without works is dead. It imperils our own life and the lives of our neighbors, whom Jesus calls us to love as we do ourselves.

I don't mean to suggest that the Bible is merely a moral playbook.

Neither is God simply a human invention, designed to reflect our values or meet our need for an imaginary coach who will help us win the game of life. The Bible is a library of sacred books that chronicle one people's search for and encounter with the divine. In addition to history, poetry, prophecy, and wisdom, it also tells the mythic story of life's beginning and consummation, as interpreted and reinterpreted by the Jewish people over time. By casting on heavenly waters their experience of the greatest and most powerful things they knew, they caught a glimpse of the holy.

The ancient Jews (including Jesus) hold an honored place along the continuum of God-diviners. This continuum begins with the cave dwellers, hunters and gatherers for whom the greatest imaginable powers were the forces of nature. "God" was manifest in fire, therefore, in lightning and in thunder—perhaps even in the game they hunted to provide sustenance. When agriculture replaced hunting and gathering, these gods turned into goddesses. Power now lay in reaping and sowing. Fecundity determined survival. God became goddess; procreation, creation; the womb, new life.

Later, with the city-state, power came wrapped in the robes of authority. God was now lord or king, protector, enforcer, and judge. A breakthrough in this view of divine nature arrived with the Hebrews, who believed their God and king was the only God and king. This development, less imperialistic than ethical, led them to attribute their failures not to another, stronger God, but to their own shortcomings. With Jesus, God became Father (in fact, Daddy, or Abba), a far more intimate authority figure.

In Western society, the God most unbelievers reject is the traditional Judeo-Christian God: omniscient, omnipotent, just, demanding, capricious on occasion, sometimes even cruel. For many thoughtful people this God was overthrown centuries ago, aided by the Copernican revolution. God was not therefore dead, as some attested; God was reimagined. For instance, after Copernicus had displaced humans from the center of the universe, one group of scientists and theologians, in their efforts to reimagine God, seized on a metaphor better suited to their new worldview. Enter God the watchmaker, who created the world and set it ticking, then withdrew to another corner of the cosmos. This is the God of the deists, a God icy and remote, still transcendent but no longer personal.

Today we are witnesses to another scientific revolution, one as profound as that initiated by Copernicus and Galileo half a millennium ago. On our path to a twenty-first-century theology, we encounter what might best be called a reflexive God, a cocreator with us in an unfolding, intricate drama of hitherto unimaginable complexity. This God is not immutable but ever-changing, -reaching, and -growing, even as we change, reach, and grow. No longer merely actors on God's stage, we may also be participants in the scripting of God's drama.

Each of our cells contains the full genetic coding or DNA for our whole being, another telling metaphor for the reflexive nature of divinity. The same idea echoes throughout the world's great scriptures. The realm of God is in a mustard seed. The Father and I are one. Atman (individual consciousness) and Brahman (universal consciousness) are one. The realm of God is within you. Not to mention Saint Paul's image of the church (one body, many members, each member endowed with equal respect). Such metaphors for God's reflexive nature transform our relationship not only with the divine, but with each other as well. Spun out of star stuff, illumined by God, we participate in the miracle we ponder.

A like image from contemporary theology underlies the Gaia hypothesis, with Mother Earth reprising the goddess in a new way. Just as every organism is a colony of cells and organs each marked with the same DNA, might not everything that lives be said to create a larger organism marked with the DNA of God? Yet another approach, that of process theology, responds to such horrors as the Holocaust by tempering the claims of God's omnipotence and omniscience. By this reading, as cocreator of a reality we share, God suffers with us when we suffer and rejoices when we experience honest joy. This is a view shared by many liberation theologians as well.

If myth projects human experience on a divine screen, parable is the discovery of the divine within the ordinary. The former is work of the mind, the latter that of the heart. When Jesus speaks of the Realm of God, he often begins his parables, "The Realm of God is like a man [or a woman] who... "—perhaps a woman who kneads bread, or a man who buries treasure in a field. If made explicit by Jesus, this kind of identification can also be found in his Jewish tradition. Early in the book of Genesis, when Abraham and Sarah accept God, God becomes part of their very names, which are changed from Abram (the people's father) to Abraham, and from Sara to Sarah (in each case, the *h* representing two of the letters of YHWH, the symbol for God).

In parable we find evidence of the divine within ordinary things and in daily encounters. The surest way to find the sacred is to decode our own experiences, not only of beauty ("heaven in a wildflower") but also in sacraments of pain by which we commune. We all suffer. We are broken and in need of healing. We struggle to accept ourselves and forgive others. To adopt the old language, we are all sinners. Aware of our imperfections, we seek more perfect faith, hope, love, and justice. At our best, we empathize with each other's pain and rise together in answer to a higher law. Illumination shines from heart to heart. We discover the healing and saving power of the holy within the ordinary. Anyone, for instance, who embraces the most familiar universalist definition of the holy, that "God is love," discovers God's nature in his or her own experience of love. This may not mean that God actually is love, but it certainly suggests that love is divine.

In our encounters with others but also with nature and art, we sometimes experience moments of peace and wholeness that reflect more eloquently than any theology the underlying basis of our relationship to the ground of our being. What the religious liberal knows, illiberal seekers, in their obsession with orthodoxy, often overlook: we are most likely to discover God when we allow our minds to follow our hearts. If God is love, which is as good a metaphor as any, then how we love measures our knowledge of God's true nature and our closeness to God more tellingly than anything we may think or believe.

In sharp contrast, some theologians treat God as a cosmic butterfly, whom they capture, kill, and pin to a board for closer observation. Skeptics then point out that God is dead. However beautiful its wings, the concept just won't fly. Whether biblical or antibiblical, both groups are peopled by hard-bitten literalists, taxidermists of the creation, wholly lacking an eye for the poetry of God.

Theology is not a science, but an art. Think of the creation as a masterpiece, the most nuanced and unfathomable masterpiece of all. As with any great work of art, interpretations concerning its meaning will differ. The greater the work, the more spirited and contentious the debate will be. This is certainly true of religion, where the task, in large measure, is to ponder the creation and make sense of it.

To understand religious passions, one can strike an analogy between competing schools of religious interpretation and those passionate little conventicles of literary critics who people our academies. For instance, while many scholars consider *Moby Dick* a masterpiece, perhaps the greatest work of American literature, to explain its meaning they offer up a myriad of interpretations: symbolist, Marxist, existentialist, deconstructionist, Jungian, Freudian, and structuralist, to name but a few.

Herman Melville was a backbencher of All Souls Unitarian Church in New York City, the congregation I serve. (A more proper and successful writer, William Cullen Bryant, served on the board of trustees and occupied a front pew.) One day, hoping to help illuminate the theology in *Moby Dick*, some enterprising Melville scholar will immerse herself in the sermons given by his pastor, Henry Whitney Bellows. She'll probably even learn a little something new (perhaps that Ishmael is the one great universalist character in nineteenth-century American literature). Then she'll write a highly detailed monograph. However brilliant, neither her "Unitarian-inflected" nor any other interpretation of *Moby Dick* will ever be complete. The book is much too rich and vast for any interpretation or cluster of interpretations to comprehend its meaning.

If *Moby Dick* and other masterpieces continue to resist final explication, that the creation, the greatest and most impenetrable masterpiece of all, should prove a far thornier text is hardly surprising. Rifling through Bellows's sermons may teach us little about Melville's theology, but the same exercise would teach us even less, in a bankable sense, about God. Bellows was one of the finest, most thoughtful liberal Christian preachers of his day, but like every other preacher, regardless of theological stripe or mental gift, he, too, was outmastered by the overwhelming nature of the task.

When interpreting any creative work, whether a novel or the cosmos, the difficulty of the critic's burden rises with the intellectual and emotional complexity of the text. When the text is the creation (especially given that we are a part of what we are attempting to interpret), an almost unfathomable level of difficulty is further compounded by the anxiety implicit in the great religious questions. People with differing interpretations of *Moby Dick* may disagree with each other, but their arguments are nothing when compared to how those with differing interpretations of the creation act when facing off in the religious arena. After all, salvation seems at stake. A handful of literary critics may believe that their interpretation of a masterpiece alone is correct, but most will acknowledge the possibility of competing truths, dealing throughout in truth with a small *t*. When it comes to God, fundamentalists insist on the absolute truth of their opinion.

In stark contrast, liberal theology is grounded on the principles of humility and openness. When we attain humility, the more we know of life and death and God the greater our ignorance appears. Beyond every ridge lies another slope and beyond every promontory looms yet another vast and awesome range. However far we trek, while cursed (or blessed) with the knowledge of our own mortality, we shall never finally know the answer to the question why.

Yet openness is rewarded. If we can never unwrap the mystery at life's core, we can nonetheless enrich our lives immensely by divining hints of the holy. Whether the hints we garner are closer to the truth than the claimed assurance of fundamentalists will reflect itself in the comparative reverence of our response to the creation. One can surely say that a faith that saves expresses its reverence differently than a faith that saves and damns.

Universalism presents a loving God, suffering and struggling with us in our attempts to be kinder, more understanding people. Such a God is not an autocrat but a democrat; not judgmental but forgiving; not ideological but flexible. Such a God values cooperation over competition; relationship over hierarchy; peace over war; neighborliness over tribalism. Such a God doesn't divide people but helps bring them together. And one way we come together is by slowly recognizing that it is God's will to beat swords into plowshares and spears into pruning hooks.

Most organized religion contains a universalist dimension, often placed somewhere near its heart. To love your neighbor as yourself (a refrain, if differently worded, of many world religions) is a universalist first principle. Yet how often religion expresses itself in language and actions expressive of neighborly hate. Within the very faiths that in their fundamentalist manifestations compete by damning each other's beliefs and communicants, Islamic, Christian, and Jewish universalists awaken to the fact that we share as human beings much more than should ever divide us. In a pluralistic world, the best we can hope for is the development of a meaningful commitment to our own faith, while acknowledging that those who believe differently may, in their own distinctive ways, be just as close to God or truth as we are. Given where we begin—in a world more divided than united by religion—the best we can hope for would be no small accomplishment. Achieve it and we shall be much better neighbors in the magnificent Cathedral of the World.

CHAPTER 2

Mother God

By my definition, the good mother is liberal by nature—generous, open-hearted, endlessly giving. Religious conservatives, "pro-family" and explicitly antiliberal in their ideology, make no room for motherhood in their Godhead: they turn to God the Father instead. In our ecologically sensitive age, the divine female, procreator and keeper of the creation, offers a dimension to the holy that seems both natural and more obvious than it has since before the city-state, when goddesses ruled over the rites of sowing and reaping, of birth and death.

Conservatives are not the only ones whose heartstrings are easily plucked by a sentimental reference to motherhood. I was certainly moved when tears welled in the eyes of a 250-pound linebacker who, after a particularly brilliant performance on the football field, confessed to a national television audience that he owed everything to his mother.

He was probably right. Abandoned by his father at an early age, he, along with his brothers and sisters, had been raised by his mother. She nurtured him and sacrificed for him, taught him the difference between right and wrong, was always there for him. He may be numbered among the fortunate ones. Denied proper childcare, education, and job training, many of his friends fell through the cracks. They are not dead or in jail or working the drug lanes because of liberal permissiveness. Quite the contrary. Lured by the sirens of Madison Avenue filling the airwaves with dream visions of fast cars, slick shoes, and hot women, they chased the American dream into the only alley available to them. Once trapped there, even their mothers couldn't save them.

If you want to protect a mother, you must first protect her children. One famous American liberal, Julia Ward Howe, reminded us of this more than a century ago. In 1870, five years after the cessation of hostilities between North and South, the Franco-Prussian War broke out in Europe. A senseless conflict, it galvanized a small but growing band of international peace activists. Director of the Perkins School for the Blind in Boston, founder of the first American women ministers group, popular poet, and author of "The Battle Hymn of the Republic," Howe, who as an abolitionist had strongly supported the Union cause, now figured prominently among the American crusaders for peace.

She wrote a manifesto against the Franco-Prussian War, had it translated into five languages (French, German, Italian, Spanish, and Swedish), and then set out for Europe intending to deliver it at international peace conferences in London and Paris. But because she was a woman, the European organizers denied her a place on the program. Angry but undaunted, she hired her own hall, and posted broadsides inviting the public to hear her. Few people came. So she returned to the United States, not broken but inspired with a new idea. She called it Mother's Day.

Howe designed Mother's Day to draw attention to several basic liberal values. Her object was not to put mothers on a pedestal. She wanted to draw mothers out of their kitchens and parlors and into the public square, to unite as many women as possible in a common cause: the protection of children from war. Or, as she put it, "to promote the alliance of the different nationalities, the amicable settlement of international questions, the great and general interests of peace." Significantly, she didn't call her annual festival International Peace Day; she called it Mother's Day, knowing no group that could more naturally or persuasively sponsor an annual festival of love and peace.

On June 2, 1870, Howe issued the first Mother's Day proclamation. She encouraged "all women who have hearts, whether your baptism be that of water or of tears," to say firmly:

> We will not have great questions decided by irrelevant agencies. Our husbands shall not come to us, reeking with carnage, for caresses and applause. Our sons shall not be taken from us to unlearn all that we have been able to teach them of charity, mercy and patience. We women of one country will be too tender of those of another country to allow our sons to be trained to injure theirs. From the bosom of the devastated earth a voice goes up with our own. It says "Disarm, Disarm! The sword of murder is not the balance of justice."

Linking motherhood, Mother Earth, womanhood, and peace, Howe asserted that the unconditional love they hold for their children invests mothers with a natural and deep interest in preventing bloodshed. Fathers send their sons to war; mothers remain at home to grieve. Who could better symbolize the need for peace than any soldier's mother? Mother's Day would remind everyone that the world would be a better place if we all rose to the challenge of motherhood: nurturing life, fostering love, giving peace a chance. "Let women now leave all that may be left of home for a great and earnest day of counsel," she proclaimed. "Let them meet first, as women, to bewail and commemorate the dead. Let them then solemnly take counsel with each other as to the means whereby the great human family can live in peace, each bearing after his own time the sacred impress, not of Caesar, but of God."

For several years, on June 2, in New York, Boston, and Philadelphia (also in England, Scotland, and Switzerland), Mother's Day was celebrated in this spirit. As with many of our national festivals, it has fallen on hard times. What began as a celebration of the second great commandment (to love thy neighbor as thyself) has devolved into a commercial holiday cosponsored by the florist and greeting-card industries. Rather than calling on mothers to unite, rally, march, and proclaim to the world the values they so liberally bestow on their children, we celebrate their domesticity with flowers and clichéd rhymes.

Julia Ward Howe had it right. What good mothers have in common is not that they stay at home with the children. Far more importantly, they instill in those same children a respect for others, generosity of spirit, cooperation, forgiveness, and loving-kindness— fundamental liberal values.

I can't speak about mothers in general without saying a few words about my own mother. If all good mothers are generic liberals, my mother takes the cake. She slips easily into almost every adjective that adorns the term: openhearted and open-minded to be sure, but permissive and profligate as well.

Her name is Bethine, a name coined from "be thine," and that's the way she's lived her life, for others. But also for herself. As those women know who have given themselves away without return, to love your neighbor as yourself can be a cruel adage. As with many women, any superficial description of my mother makes her sound like someone else's property. The daughter of a governor. The wife of a U.S. senator. This is wildly misleading. Actually she's the best politician in the family, knowing better than any of us that "politics is people." She certainly would have understood and rallied to Julia Ward Howe's vision of Mother's Day.

My mother even saved me from the bomb. It was 1958. Fire drills in elementary school had been temporarily replaced by nuclear-attack drills. The alarm would go off and send all of us scurrying to tuck ourselves under our desks. From the moment of the first alert to the arrival of the pretend missiles, we had ten minutes. Three times a year we practiced this. I can assure you (and some of you will remember), ten minutes pass very slowly when you are crouching under your desk waiting for an imaginary nuclear bomb to fall.

So I planned my escape, and practiced by running home after school every day. Despite an innate lack of athletic ability, I finally completed the trip in under ten minutes. One day I arrived panting at the door, and my mother, fearing that once again I had attracted the attention of neighborhood bullies, asked me why I was so winded. I told her of my plan. She understood completely. "If there ever were a nuclear attack, I'd want you here with me, not at school under your stupid desk," she said.

So my mother went to the principal and requested that, in the event of nuclear attack, I might have permission to run home and die with her. The result was a new school policy. If they'd secured parental permission, children who could get home within ten minutes would be excused from school should a nuclear attack take place.

Each of us learns different things from his or her parents, but there are ways in which all nurturing parents are alike. Through the unconditional gift of their love and the security offered by sheltering arms and the comforts of home, we learn to trust others and life itself. More by example than instruction, our parents also teach us how to balance freedom and responsibility, individual wants and community needs. Both are first modeled in the family, with its one body and several members.

Like the church, at one level the family is a conservative institution. It establishes boundaries, maintains tradition, and performs a stabilizing role in society. Each of these functions is noble, and the breakdown of the family is surely a distressing symptom, even a direct cause, of the breakdown of societal values.

On the other hand, within the family, the maternal role (whether performed by a mother, father, grandparent, or older sibling) is one of modeling and inculcating liberal values: hospitality, neighborliness, forgiveness, compassion, and tender-loving care. Political liberals do not possess these traits any more surely than conservatives do. Anyone can be a bad parent, regardless of his or her politics or religion. But good mothers do foster core liberal values.

Maternal love is unconditional, not proffered in exchange for good behavior. As with all tokens of liberality, it is given freely without demand for an equivalent return. Nurturing mothers do not dole out love on a point system. The prodigal child may even receive more than the dutiful one. Good mothers give their children what they deserve only in the broadest sense of the term, that of natural entitlement. Every child deserves maternal love, not because of what he or she does but because of who he or she is, a part of the human family, a child of God.

When we liken God the creator to a parent, viewing ourselves as God's children, God has traditionally worn a male persona. Outside the community of fundamentalists, most searching theologians today would not limit God by gender. But if such a limit were to be imposed, God the Mother strikes me as much more descriptive of God's possible nature than does God the Father. If the height of religious goodness lies in deeds of love and compassion, even as its nadir rests in holy war, we might wisely turn from God the Lord and Father of Mankind to God the Mother, creator, comforter, and healer. Each of these powers is no less great than the powers of sovereignty and judgment, but rather than damning, they save.

The Latin root of the word "religion" is *religere*, meaning "to bind together." Many who call themselves religious have instead narrowed their theology down to a straitjacketed literalistic system, a way to broker salvation through unqualified acceptance of a certain set of faith propositions drawn from one or another tribe's ancient story. To spell out and enforce their creeds, they employ a linear, classically male, left-brained way of thinking. The chief effect of such religion is to divide the saved from the damned, not to bind us together. Being religious in the capacious sense of the word—that which unites us as kith and kin—can be canceled out completely by belonging to a patriarchal group that believes it alone has the truth and that everyone else is damned.

How different this is from embracing the creation, where the principal books of revelation are the book of nature and the book of human nature, filled with lessons of sowing and reaping, of seeds coming to fruition, of the wonder of birth and the imperative to nurture. Mother God saves.

Think about the words we use to express compassion. We are compassionate when we console—literally, to stand beside another in his or her aloneness—when we commiserate, opening our hearts to share the misery a loved one or neighbor is going through; and when we offer comfort—the word "comfort" meaning to bring to another our strength. At heart, consolation, commiseration, and comfort are seen as feminine, not masculine, values. Men can be compassionate, too, of course, but when compassion is listed among a set of traits that people are asked to define as male or female, respondents typically place it on the distaff side of the ledger.

When God became Goddess, the greatest power was not deemed a lord or king, replete with a mighty army to quell enemies and ensure safety, but instead the renewal of the earth, in cycles of sowing and reaping. The fecund earth, Mother Earth, with her supernatural attendants, gave life, even as a mother gives life through birth and nurtures life through love. To tend the earth and keep it, not to lord over the earth, was the essence of goddess worship. God the Mother gave birth and then lavished unconditional love on her children. Today, in our ecologically focused age, the female dimension of the divine once again makes natural sense.

The cycles of nature and the miracle of birth induce a deep sense of awe, a primary constituent of universalism. Beauty surrounds us and we constantly miss it. To awaken, we must somehow rediscover our kinship with the creation. Humanitarian Albert Schweitzer spoke of this principle as reverence for life. We are a part of, not apart from, a vast and mysterious living system.

Mystics of every faith proclaim this sense of oneness. The mystical oneness of person to person, of parent to child and then brother to sister and neighbor to neighbor, is but a familiar expression of the mystical oneness of all existence in the great chain of being. Theologians may reason their way to such oneness, but mothers know it by heart. Extended from hearth to altar, this sense of cosmic kinship cannot help but uplift and transform our lives. A religion inspired by love exalts self and other alike by placing us together in divine kinship as children of one great mystery, children of God the Mother, creator, consoler, and comforter. Whenever we remember how intimately we are woven and how interdependent we truly are, we return, if not to the womb, certainly to the altar of motherhood, the altar of creation, the altar of unconditional love.

Without even meaning to, my mother taught me this. She taught me that we are all related; we are kin, members of a single human family. She herself first learned the liberal principle of neighborliness from her grandmother, whom she once called "the most ecumenical person I ever met." Speaking at the 1988 Martin Luther King celebration in Boise, Idaho, my mother told a story about her grandmother to illustrate two truths: though we are each different, at heart we are one; and, because we are different, we have a hard time understanding one another.

"My grandmother Clark was very upright and moral," my mother began. "Her favorite poem was 'No Sex in Heaven.' This title caused some confusion for me until I was old enough to read and understand that the word was spelled 's-e-c-t-s.'"

My mother spoke that day of Abraham Lincoln and the Emancipation Proclamation. She spoke of the bravery it took to march up to the schoolhouse door in Little Rock, to march for integration in the South, to defy the bans against free assembly in South Africa.

Julia Ward Howe would have been proud to hear my mother give public expression to the maternal ethic of care and tenderness. She would also have understood her choice of holidays in which to proclaim these liberal values. Today, the Martin Luther King Jr. holiday is a far more appropriate occasion for their expression than is Mother's Day in its present incarnation.

In 1913, when Congress moved the date from June 2 to the second Sunday in May, it also changed the significance of Mother's Day. What had been a festival in which mothers might witness publicly to maternal values was reduced to a private holiday on which their loved ones sent them cards and roses.

Like Julia Ward Howe, my mother got it right. Motherhood has nothing to do with pedestals, and everything to do with peace and love. As Bethine Church said in her closing words about Martin Luther King Jr.: "Let us here today and in our daily lives all be prepared to love and care about each other, to let our differences strengthen rather than diminish us. Let us give up fear of each other and change it into belief in ourselves and our ability to add healing in this often-injured world."

The liberal gospel: spoken like a true mother.

BOOK II

The American Creed

CHAPTER 3

The Role of Religion in
American Democracy

Universalism beats at the heart of the American experiment. "Out of many, one" is another way to say, "One light, many windows." With the nationalism that followed the terrorist attacks of 9/11 burning almost out of control, I revisited our founding documents and national shrines in search of true American patriotism (with liberty and justice for all). In 2002 I summarized these findings in The American Creed: A Biography of the Declaration of Independence. *Over the intervening years, I've developed this theme in two additional books and many occasional pieces. This section, exploring the relationship of core American values with universalist theology, opens with a definitional piece that I wrote at the request of Bill Sinkford, then president of the Unitarian Universalist Association, in 2007.*

According to a recent Beliefnet poll (September 2007), 55 percent of the American people believe that the United States was founded as a Christian nation. In fact, the Constitution is mum on the subject. The only mention of religion appears in the antidiscrimination clause respecting candidates for federal office. Article VI includes the stipulation that "no religious test shall ever be required as a qualification to any office or public trust under the United States."

During the debate over ratification of the Constitution, many mainline Christians howled at its silence on religion. The Presbytery of Massachusetts and New Hampshire groused to George Washington, "We should not have been alone in rejoicing to have seen some explicit acknowledgment of THE TRUE ONLY GOD, AND JESUS CHRIST whom he has sent, inserted somewhere in the Magna Charta of our country." Washington demurred. "I am persuaded, you will permit me to observe, that the path of true piety is so plain as to require but little political direction," he said. "To this consideration we ought to ascribe the absence of any regulation respecting religion from the Magna Charta of our country."

Reflected in this debate, two competing themes combined to compose the dissonant music of early American politics. The first theme, sounded in New England from the time of the Puritans, posited the ideal of a Christian commonwealth. Uplifted by the imperatives of Christian morality, the government would be a shining city on a hill, fulfilling God's mandates and receiving his aid.

The second theme, codified in Thomas Jefferson's Declaration of Independence, arose from Enlightenment France. Rather than that of Christian commonwealth, it posited the ideal of individual freedom. Jefferson dreamed of establishing an "empire for liberty," whose government would protect each individual's God-given freedom of conscience.

Both visions had religious dimensions—call them divine order and sacred liberty. Cast in terms of the nation's motto, *E pluribus unum* ("Out of many, one"), the *unum*, or divine order, people believed that, to uphold "one nation under God," the secular and sacred realms must rest on a single foundation. Without a united sense of purpose and clear moral vision, they argued, liberty would lapse into license.

Champions of sacred liberty, *pluribus* people, as it were, believed that, to promote "liberty and justice for all," the secular and religious realms must remain autonomous. Government attempts to impose religious (or moral) values suppress religion instead, they claimed, by violating individual freedom of conscience. In the early republic, the Baptist Church stood alongside Jefferson in the vanguard of those championing freedom of conscience and strict church-state separation.

The gathering consensus (from early in our history to now) unites aspects of both traditions, combining state protection of freedom of conscience with a strong tradition of moral politics. While church and state are separate under the Constitution, religion and politics mix freely in our national life.

Religion will always have a place in our politics. Religious values are, or should be, moral values. They instruct both our activism and our votes. Yet religion has thrived in America in large measure because the government was prevented from corrupting its franchise. In England, for instance, where the Anglican Church fed at the government's trough for centuries, next to nobody attends worship. The United States of America is the most religious Western industrialized nation precisely because our religious institutions have maintained their moral independence and therefore their moral authority.

If church and state operate independently under U.S. charter, American democracy is nonetheless founded on a moral pediment. Jefferson's Declaration of Independence holds us (as it did him) under moral judgment: to guarantee liberty and justice for all. So defined, there may be too little religion in today's politics, not too much. Too little of the religion prescribed by the prophet Micah: "To do justice and love mercy and walk humbly with your God." Too little of the religion taught by Rabbi Jesus, who summed up all the law and the prophets in two great commandments: "To love God with all your heart and mind and soul and your neighbor as yourself." Too little of the religion as defined by Thomas Jefferson, who said, "It is in our lives and not in our words that our religion must be read."

CHAPTER 4

The American Creed

On January 29, 2002, I delivered a keynote address to the annual theological conference at Bangor Theological Seminary in Bangor, Maine. I drew inspiration from my soon-to-be-published work, The American Creed. *These words are abstracted from that address.*

The United States of America is a liberal democracy. It is the model for all other liberal democracies. The liberal impulse, both religious and political, shaped our country from its very inception. It informed the development of religious freedom, separation of church and state, equal protection under the law, freedom of speech and press, liberal education, and a generous-spirited social contract.

In the Declaration of Independence and reconfirmed at the high points of U.S. history, our republic also confesses to a sacral center—call it the American Creed. As a people, we subscribe to the principles it affirms. This creed couples religious freedom with an encompassing national faith. In America, the common good is grounded in a set of virtues—justice, liberty, and equality—that our founders established as touchstones of the good society. Devoted to the proposition that all people are created equal and endowed with certain inalienable rights, the American Creed combats tyranny while at the same time tempering the centrifugal forces of untrammeled freedom and relativism. The aspirational ideal of a spiritual bond that protects religious liberty is our greatest achievement as a nation.

Whatever particular belief system an individual may profess, in America he or she subscribes by definition, if not always by practice, to a more universal faith. This faith secures our liberty, while tempering its excesses to ensure the common good. Catholic, Protestant, Muslim, and Jew, Buddhist, Hindu, secular humanist, and Wiccan alike draw from a common source and thereby participate in a broader moral community. To this extent, all active Americans play a civil religious role. Faith in the people to combine for the common good is an expression of the American Creed.

Religion has been a transformational force in this country precisely because at critical moments the liberal spirit challenged the complacency and revitalized the prophetic vigor of our national faith. Several of our most influential founding fathers—Benjamin Franklin, Thomas Jefferson, and John Adams—were religious liberals.

None of the founders drew a more direct correlation between God's law and our own mandate to imitate that law in building an equitable society than did Thomas Jefferson. In his Preamble to the Declaration of Independence, it is God's will that requires the establishment of liberal values in any society drawn up according to a divine blueprint. Invoking "the Laws of Nature and of Nature's God" to confirm every people's entitlement to "a separate and equal station," Jefferson expands this notion of equality from a people, or nation, to all persons: "We hold these truths to be self-evident, that all Men are created equal, that they are endowed by their Creator with certain unalienable rights, that among these are Life, Liberty, and the Pursuit of Happiness." America's egalitarian mandate reflects the liberality of the creator, and thus countermands, by divine witness, all feudal and aristocratic structures. It also parallels the Jewish concept of *tikkun olam*, or "repairing the world," which holds that the human spirit is in partnership with God to help finish the work of creation.

American civil religion has nothing in common with the civil religion defined as a social contract by the eighteenth-century French philosopher Jean-Jacques Rousseau. To Rousseau, civil religion represented a state-authorized and imposed faith, ensuring the coherence of religious uniformity to preserve public peace. Such civil religion is collective, not pluralistic, in nature. It fosters nationalism while undermining the integrity of religion itself.

In sharp contrast, American civil religion protects the integrity of particular bodies of faith, while uniting the entire people in a common moral endeavor. When weak or merely rhetorical, civil religion cannot perform its role or does so poorly. When vital, it offers a banner under which all Americans can gather. It inspires self-corrective energy to ensure that we remain mindful of and true to our national ideals. Universalist and ecumenical by definition, healthy expressions of civil religion mitigate the fragmentation of our national ethos, combat the moral attrition endemic to modernism, and secure the foundation of the common good.

The American Creed is fashioned in such a way that, at its best, civil religion in America is prophetic, standing in judgment of our performance as a people at home and as a nation abroad. Conversely, lacking the notion that we stand and therefore must place ourselves under higher judgment, public religion becomes pernicious, even dangerous, in direct proportion to our citizens' enthusiasm for it. When it feeds our collective or individual appetites rather than raising our national conscience, unself-critical public faith turns freedom itself into an idol. It also fosters tyranny. Flags have been waved and Bibles thumped in defense of every manner of immorality and amorality, from slavery (defended on the basis of biblical authority, states' rights, and national precedent) to American imperialism.

A public square that polices itself against sectarian religious co-option need not be restricted to the banalities of unself-critical national chauvinism. Expressions of American faith (as broadly defined and understood by our founders) not only should be permitted in the public square, but should also be welcomed. When tuned to the highest anthems of our history, they offer a needful corrective to both relativist and fundamentalist pieties.

Historians debate the extent of American "exceptionalism," but several facts are clear. As nineteenth-century French social critic Alexis de Tocqueville pointed out, "America [is] the only country in which the starting-point of a people has been clearly observable." Our first European ancestors didn't come here without a text, but they wrote on a new slate. Little more than two centuries after the Pilgrim landing at Plymouth, Tocqueville, traveling on an educational tour of America, wrote to a friend back in France, "Picture to yourself...if you can, a society which comprises all the nations of the world...people differing from one another in language, in beliefs, in opinions, in a word, a society possessing no roots, no memories, no prejudices, no routine, no common ideas, no national character.... This, then, is our starting point! What is the connecting link between these so different elements? How are they welded into one people?"

Tocqueville answered his own question in his magisterial two-volume study, *Democracy in America*, published in 1835. America was less diverse back then than it is today. But it already possessed, as Tocqueville discovered, a distinct set of national ideas and an identifiable national character. However tragically for the indigenous peoples they found here, from the moment the first Pilgrims arrived on these shores America as we know it began to be inscribed with self-conscious intent.

Drawing on this past, what our founders gave birth to in 1776 was something unique in the history of human governance. No one has expressed this more clearly than another visitor from abroad, the British novelist and philosopher G. K. Chesterton: "America is the only nation in the world that is founded on a creed. That creed is set forth with dogmatic and even theological lucidity in the Declaration of Independence....It enunciates that all men are equal in their claim to justice, and that governments exist to give them that justice, and that their authority is for that reason just."

In his essay "What Is America?" Chesterton asks, "What makes America peculiar?" America is "a home for the homeless," he concludes, welcoming people from everywhere in the world. What makes America peculiar is the "idea of making a new nation literally out of [people from] any old nation that comes along." This is certainly part of the answer. When one moves to Japan, one doesn't become Japanese, any more than a person who chooses to live in Greece (the cradle of democracy) becomes Greek, or another becomes French when he or she moves to Paris (where revolution broke out in 1789, the very year George Washington was sworn in as president of the United States).

The other characteristic Chesterton found unique to America is that ours is "a nation with the soul of a church." Though the American Creed as fashioned by Thomas Jefferson and his colleagues insists on a clear separation between church and state, this in no way suggests that the body politic is lacking a religious soul. Chesterton was of the opinion that the American Creed "certainly does condemn anarchism, and it does also by inference condemn atheism, since it clearly names the Creator as the ultimate authority from whom these equal rights are derived." The saving irony, which Chesterton appears to have missed, is that this same creed also protects atheists against the coercion of believers.

More profoundly than Chesterton did, a third foreign observer, the Swedish sociologist Gunnar Myrdal, recognized the all-encompassing and self-correcting nature of what he, too, called "the American Creed." Of the documents in which it is contained, Myrdal writes, "the schools teach them. The churches preach them. The courts pronounce their judicial decisions in their terms." We teach this creed to correct our nation's course as well as to celebrate it. Because our founders did not and we have yet to fulfill our creed's promise, "America," Myrdal concludes, "is continuously struggling for its soul." Martin Luther King Jr. echoed Myrdal when he had a dream "that one day this nation will rise up and live out the true meaning of its creed."

When the Carnegie Foundation first asked him to do a study of America, Myrdal conceded that "America has had gifted conservative statesmen and national leaders...But with few exceptions, only the liberals have gone down in history as national heroes." Small wonder, for as the dictionary reminds us, "liberal" means free: free from narrow prejudice; open-minded, candid; free from unreasonable prejudice in favor of traditional opinions or established institutions; open to the reception of new ideas or proposals of reform; and, of political opinions, favorable to legal or administrative reforms tending in the direction of freedom or democracy. "Liberal" and "freedom" *are* synonymous: freedom from bondage; freedom for opportunity; and freedom with responsibility, especially toward our neighbor, whose rights and security are just as precious as our own. When the narrow sympathies of some and the fear of others combine to mute this generous cry, we must give it new voice.

To reanimate this voice requires recapturing the liberal spirit. I say recapture, because the liberal spirit, which is the American spirit, finds its most eloquent expression in symbols that have been ceded to or co-opted by the religious and political right.

Let's start with the flag. It is one thing to wrap oneself in the flag, but those who do—and indeed those of us who reactively do not—might consider what it actually means to pledge allegiance to the republic for which it stands: "I pledge allegiance to the flag of the United States of America, and to the republic for which it stands, one nation under God [the words "under God" were added to the original pledge in 1954], indivisible, with liberty and justice for all."

This language captures the true spirit of the American hope. So how have those who remained faithful to this spirit managed to get themselves branded as being "anti-American"? Not simply by championing unpopular social programs in a selfish age: that's too convenient and self-flattering an answer. The real reason is this: many liberals have relinquished the very symbols that speak most persuasively to the American heart. To make matters worse, they ceded these symbols to those who have their finger on its pulse but cannot feel its noble beat.

Listen to the American Creed as it rings in Franklin Delano Roosevelt's words: "The basic things expected by our people of their political and economic systems are simple. They are equality of opportunity for youth and for others; jobs for those who can work; security for those who need it; the ending of special privilege for the few; the preservation of civil liberties for all; ... Our nation has placed its destiny in the hands and hearts of its millions of free men and women, and its faith in freedom under the guidance of God. Freedom means the supremacy of human rights everywhere."

This, from his "four freedoms" address, is a call not to American arms but to American ideals. President Roosevelt's words chime in concert not only with our Pledge of Allegiance, but also with the scriptural passage our founders engraved on the Liberty Bell, taken from the book of Leviticus: "Proclaim liberty throughout the land to all the inhabitants thereof."

The Liberty Bell, the Pledge of Allegiance: if one were looking for symbols to help explain the power Franklin Roosevelt's words and ideas held for the American people, one need look no further.

Tocqueville and Chesterton were Catholics; Myrdal a self-described humanist; King an American Baptist clergyman with universalist theological leanings; and Roosevelt a liberal Episcopalian. Each considered the United States of America to be founded on and sustained by our aspirational obedience to an explicit creed. Following in their spirit, the American Creed can perhaps best be defined as a union of faith and freedom in which faith elevates freedom and freedom both protects and tempers faith.

The American Creed doesn't impose parochial faith on the commonweal, but protects freedom, including freedom of religion, by invoking a more universal authority. Employing the language of faith, it transcends all religious particulars, uniting all our citizens in a shared covenant. As important, it protects freedom from itself, tempering excesses of individual license by postulating a higher moral code.

The distinctive way in which faith and freedom unite in America secures our nation's religious spirit not within, but outside, church walls. A majority of American citizens perceive no fundamental conflict between the practice of their own individual religious beliefs and the latitude given to their neighbors to worship as they choose. At our best, we celebrate both what sets us apart (specific doctrinal conviction) and what holds us together (the American Creed).

Obviously there are people in our nation (fundamentalists of the right and left) who struggle more with such ambiguity than the average American citizen does. Seeking either to expand the compass of their personal belief system or to remove every vestige of piety from the public square, their passion shapes the national debate both on church and state and on religion and politics. Negative print images of each other, advocates for a Christian or a secularist vision of America alike misread the script of our creed.

Those who consider America a Christian nation betray the spirit of our founders. The American Creed treats Christian and non-Christian alike, offering the same protection under law, while securing equal freedom both of and from religion.

Misrepresenting American history and threatening to betray its promise, Christian fundamentalists call for a return to what they proclaim to be our founders' faith. They excoriate our nation for its loss of values, often persuasive in their critique but misguided in their understanding of the American way and of American history. Mirroring the rhetoric of Islamic terrorist leaders, some have gone so far as to see God's hand in the attack on America, as punishment for our nation's liberal social policies. By viewing our present struggle in terms of God's avenging wrath against our nation's godlessness, American fundamentalists unwittingly foster the same climate that promotes jihad.

Adamant secularists are equally wrongheaded. Secularism can mean "outside the church" (unrelated to religious conviction and institutions). But as an "ism" (or ideology) it suggests a rejection of or hostility toward religion. Taken in this sense, secularism dates from the French Revolution, not the American one.

In today's academic circles it is fashionable to argue that all opinions are of equal value (except, perhaps, the opinion that "all opinions are *not* of equal value"). It is likewise fashionable to argue that there are no overarching stories or visions of the good life through which our lives acquire meaning. Yet it is precisely the vacuum created when we forget our own nation's creed that invites occupation by the new fundamentalists.

Academic relativists argue that invoking the abstract notions of justice and truth to support our cause won't be effective, because our adversaries lay claim to the same language. Instead, the American literary theorist Stanley Fish urges us to "fall back on the democratic ideals we embrace." Yet these very ideals enshrine a radically different truth (an overarching vision, if you will) than that espoused by the fundamentalists who sponsor terror. If we lack the heart, faith, and courage to reclaim and model the "self-evident" truths on which our nation was established, we will remain vulnerable to those whose religious rhetoric fills the spiritual void we have left in abandoning the creed of our founders.

Organized religion frightens many Americans, and for good reason. Our world is rife with religious terrorists. And the stakes are high, for salvation is at stake. When true believers confront neighbors who believe differently than they do or who don't believe in God at all, they have (unless they are convinced by their neighbors' arguments) only four options. They can attempt to (1) convert, (2) destroy, (3) ignore, or (4) respect those who hold contrasting views.

Fundamentalism embraces the first and, in its most radical expression, the second of these four options. Secularism occasionally imposes the second—witness the gulags—but most widely embraces the third. The American way, charted by our forebears and coded in the spirit of our nation's laws, represents the fourth path. The spirit of liberal democracy—with respect given to the worth and dignity of every individual, and minority rights protected insofar as the commonweal can still be maintained—celebrates religious pluralism.

Branding America "the great Satan," Osama bin Laden proclaimed that it was God himself who attacked the World Trade Center and the Pentagon. America is caricatured throughout much of the Muslim world as a godless society wedded to materialism and wanton in the exercise of its power around the globe. In the struggle against terrorism, being true to our ideals will be more effective than taking up arms. Historically, the most effective way to counter a narrow creed is by fulfilling the mandates of a broader one. To remain true to her highest values, America must reembody the ideals of democratic pluralism, not insist on the vaunted superiority of modern capitalism. The conservative columnist George F. Will is correct when he writes that the terrorists "hate America because it is the purest expression of modernity—individualism, pluralism, freedom, secularism." But, save for pluralism and freedom, this is an America watered down from the rich mead of our founders. To survive the assault of neotribalism, America will have to revisit her shrines and recover her soul.

By definition, as confirmed by the Declaration of Independence and elaborated in our federal Constitution and Bill of Rights, ours is a union of faith and freedom. Neither alone could be half as redemptive as the two are together. The American Creed finds its highest expression in the devotion we render at once to liberty and to union. So defined, American religious *fundamentals* are as lucid as the convictions of Christian *fundamentalists*. But they are religious in a different way, one that reflects the expansive faith of our founders. As an indication of its breadth, this faith was placed in the people themselves. Our founders were dedicated to individual religious rights, not to the imposition of a specific set of religious doctrines. To this extent, they placed a greater trust in both God and the people than fundamentalists do. Implicit in democratic pluralism is the belief that liberty can be an agent of truth, and that truth cannot be coerced.

The founders also recognized that freedom is a morally neutral quality, defined by the objects to which it is devoted. Without a moral mooring, our liberties run the risk of lapsing into license. When this happens, fundamentalists and other people of faith are right to be alarmed. The American Creed doesn't play favorites when it comes to theology—again, atheists receive the same protections fundamentalists do. But it does rest on a moral foundation. To abridge people's religious freedom cuts against the American grain, but no more destructively than to exercise freedom without a sense of moral responsibility. To invoke the American Creed, as Abraham Lincoln did, is to call our nation under the judgment of an authority higher than sect, mammon, or self-interest.

One saving grace of the American people is our optimism. When transfigured by faith, this optimism is elevated to hope. Hope's refrain is a dominant chord in the nation's history, present most tellingly at times of greatest trial. "I believe that we are lost here in America," the novelist Thomas Wolfe wrote, "but I believe we shall be found.... I think the true discovery of America is before us. I think the true fulfillment of our spirit, of our people, of our mighty and immortal land, is yet to come. I think the true discovery of our own democracy is still before us."

If the true discovery of our democracy is before us, to speed that day's arrival we must revisit its sacred text. The American Creed is an ethical will entrusted to succeeding generations by the founders to advance the quest they began that witheringly hot July two and a quarter centuries ago, with the signing of the Declaration of Independence. If we follow in their footsteps and beyond, their dream for America will come true and the grail of faith and freedom will be ours.

CHAPTER 5

What Would Jefferson Do?

John Adams and Thomas Jefferson together embody the Declaration of Independence, the former as the document's most compelling sponsor, the latter as its author—then together through the stirring coincidence of their both dying on July 4, 1826, fifty years to the day it was published. On July Fourth, to keep our nation on its original keel, we might do well to ask, "What would Jefferson (and Adams) do?" a question put to me by Chris Walton, then editor of the UU World, *who ran the following answer to commemorate the holiday in 2006, shortly before the publication of my book on religion and the founders,* So Help Me God: The Founding Fathers and the First Great Battle over Church and State.

With religious politics contributing to the fireworks this Independence Day weekend, what might John Adams and Thomas Jefferson have to say if they were to pay a surprise visit to the twenty-first-century United States?

Theologically, the second and third U.S. presidents were unitarians: Adams, a member of the Quincy, Massachusetts, congregation; Jefferson, a sect unto himself. Apart from their congenial theological views, from the moment they collaborated in founding the nation until both retired from politics, they disagreed on almost everything else.

In their retirement, however, they began a long correspondence about history, religion, and politics that, even as it healed old wounds, brings new delight to almost anyone who chances to dip into it two centuries later.

Not long before their bravura final act—dying hours apart on the fiftieth anniversary of their supreme joint achievement, the signing of the Declaration of Independence on the Fourth of July, 1776—the two old political combatants mused wistfully about the future. How fascinating it would be, they wrote, if they could "drop in" every now and then to see how the "American experiment" was faring.

Were they to choose this particular holiday weekend for a visit, Adams would find the religious nationalism proclaimed in many pulpits familiar, perhaps even to his liking. Although he drifted from the doctrines of his ancestors, religiously (though not theologically) Adams remained, at heart, a Puritan. As leader of the law-and-order Federalist Party, he devoutly believed that the republic must be founded on strong Christian principles. Besides, he loved going to church. Even so, if after worship he were to drop by the White House, he might offer his latest successor a lesson on the dangers of religious politics.

As the election of 1800 drew near, Adams faced a looming electoral rematch against Jefferson, his vice president and political enemy. The Federalists derided the politically potent Virginian as an "atheist" (untrue), a "deist" (true), and a "Jacobin" (i.e., "French radical," also true). The Federalists summed up their two greatest nightmares, atheism and popular democracy, by hurling the epithet "Jacobin" at their opponents.

Adams had no sympathy for the French Revolution. Years later, he looked back bitterly on the "hot, rash, blind, headlong, furious efforts to ameliorate the condition of society, to establish liberty, equality, fraternity, and the rights of man." Adams especially scorned Democratic-Republicans like Jefferson who admired the revolutionary French Republic.

The Democratic-Republicans wore French colors (cocked hats with a knot of red, white, and blue ribbons pinned to the side), in saucy contrast to the less frivolous black cockades Federalist stalwarts wore, harking back to Revolutionary days. To Federalist eyes, Demo-cratic-Republicans with their tricolor cockades had taken the Fourth of July hostage by drawing undue attention to the Preamble of the Declaration of Independence. In writing the Declaration, Jeffer-son had introduced three lofty principles (the right to liberty, God-given equality, and popular sovereignty) and one incendiary one (the people's authority to overthrow their government). The Federalists' problem, as they themselves soon recognized, lay in the Declaration of Independence itself.

Early in Adams's presidency, proper Philadelphians boycotted In-dependence Day, which might as well have been Bastille Day as far as the local Federalists were concerned. Nary a black cockade was to be seen on the anniversary of the nation's birth. Many church bells remained silent. And every reveler crowding Independence Square was indecently festooned in heretical red, white, and blue. In New England, separate tricolor and black cockade Fourth of July celebra-tions became the rule. In their orations, Federalist preachers and pol-iticians dedicated their energies on the nation's birthday to critique the un-American, anti-Christian dogma that Jefferson so impudently inserted into the nation's founding document. In his Boston Inde-pendence Day oration in 1799, John Lowell warned his listeners to beware "the seductive doctrines of 'Liberty' and 'Equality.'"

The year before, Alexander Hamilton had no difficulty convinc-ing Adams that for the government to proclaim a national fast day, a federal request honored by all the churches that chose to participate, would galvanize his more conservative Federalist political base. In-deed it did. Raising a host of traditional black cockades, hundreds of New England preachers seized this governmentally sanctioned op-portunity to pronounce French and Jeffersonian infidelity a demonic double threat to the future of America's Christian republic.

Later in life, Adams looked back ruefully on his decision to pro-mote a religious event for political gain. He went so far as to claim that it cost him the presidency. For one thing, it left the plausible impression that he had buckled under pressure from Presbyterian church leaders, who urgently were calling for the president to pro-claim a day of national worship.

Declaring a national fast was like poking a stick into a nest of hornets. In alarm, dissenting Christians (Baptists, Methodists, and the like) howled that Adams was compromising church-state separation. For sound religious reasons, not only did they boycott the fast day, but they also came out in droves to support Jefferson, the more secular candidate. "Nothing is more dreaded than the national government meddling with religion," Adams concluded in 1812, years too late to save him from his ill-calculated experiment in Christian governance. I suspect, for all his piety, that Adams would want subsequent presidents to grasp this insight, too.

Jefferson would likely not join Adams for worship to inaugurate his return visit, but he might pop into a bookstore. Leafing through any contemporary biography, this intensely private man would find to his chagrin that his personal compilation from the Gospels—he excerpted Jesus's life and teachings while excluding the virgin birth, miracles, and resurrection—had entered the public domain under the title *The Jefferson Bible*. (He might even chastise me for being among those who have introduced the text to a modern-day audience.) He would as quickly discover that his best-remembered religious prophecy—that every child born in his enlightened time "would die a Unitarian"—had landed miles from the mark.

Jefferson's personal pursuit of painlessness led him to anesthetize his conscience (tragically so with respect to slavery) whenever it caused him discomfort. But on the Fourth of July, he got America right. The Declaration of Independence elevated people's sights by placing human law on a higher moral pediment. The result was a civil ethic in which the ideals of liberty and equality received unprecedented priority. In his draft of the Preamble, the truths that we know as "unalienable" Jefferson described as "sacred and undeniable." The transcendent point of reference was no longer the monarch but the people themselves, whose rights he endowed with sovereign, even divine, authority. Individuals thus became ends in themselves, not means by which to advance some other agent's ends. In his view, far from compromising faith, this emphasis on liberty perfected faith by ceding it full range. In its ringing, redemptive moral urgency, Jefferson's Preamble is rightly remembered as the American Creed.

Whatever may be trumpeted from the nation's pulpits this Independence Day weekend, preachers who confuse the Christian church with the American state, as President John Adams so fatefully did, toy recklessly with the founders' Declaration. To paraphrase that covenant in words that every patriot should be proud to hymn in unison, the home of the brave is also the land of the free.

CHAPTER 6

America's Promise

Given the ennobling chords contained in the nation's creed, we may reasonably ask why we so often get it wrong. On slavery, women's rights, and indigenous sovereignty, even our founders got it wrong. Their gift to us, and challenge to themselves, was to establish our nation on a high moral pediment, one that would hold us under judgment to the end of our days. However mixed our deeds, the story of our nation is nonetheless a tale of gradual moral progress, in which deed begins to approximate creed. These words are taken from the final chapter of The American Creed.

Not long ago, Roger Wilkins, nephew of the civil rights leader Roy Wilkins and a professor of American history at George Mason University, visited the Jefferson Memorial. Standing beneath the dome of a monument dedicated to the memory of one of America's most honored slave owners, Wilkins brooded on Jefferson's complicity in his family's bondage. Then those immortal words recorded on a single slab of marble rang out their saving message. He could not help but marvel at "the throbbing phrases at the core of the American hymn to freedom that Jefferson composed and flung out against the sky."

Roger Wilkins is an American. Like all Americans, he participates in a yet-unfinished story. This story is both noble and tragic, but its genius is emblazoned from the beginning. "The Declaration of Independence," Wilkins concluded, "for all the ambiguity around it, constitutes the Big Bang in the physics of freedom and equality in America."

Unlike the Constitution, the Declaration is so explicit in its language that slavery proponents finally had to reject it. In 1861 the vice president of the Confederate States of America, Alexander Stephens, conceded that the Declaration proclaims liberty and equality for all and that Jefferson himself believed slavery to be in violation of the laws of nature. Jefferson's ideas "were fundamentally wrong," Stephens proclaimed. "Our new government is founded upon exactly the opposite idea; its foundations are laid; its corner-stone rests, upon the great truth that the negro is not equal to the white man; that slavery, subordination to the superior race, is his natural and normal condition." Stephens once had quoted Proverbs 25:11 to Abraham Lincoln—"A word fitly spoken is like apples of gold in pictures of silver." Here is Lincoln's reply.

> The expression of that principle ["all men are created equal"] in our Declaration of Independence was the word "fitly spoken" which has proved an "apple of gold" to us. The Union and the Constitution are the picture of silver subsequently framed around it. The picture was made not to conceal or destroy the apple; but to adorn and preserve it. The picture was made for the apple, not the apple for the picture. So let us act, that neither picture nor apple shall ever be blurred, bruised or broken.

From the outset of the American experiment, our nation's leaders attempted to set a new mark. The meaning of our history sounds as clearly from the nobility of their ideals as it does in the incomplete fulfillment of their promise. To be a moral people is not to be a perfect people. (Otherwise there would be no such thing as morality, perfection stifling every effort to ensure its attainment.) But the founders saw to it that we would hold ourselves to a higher standard. "An almost chosen people," in Lincoln's words, we demonstrate our greatness not by force of might or by virtue of our unquestioned economic dominance, but through rigorous moral endeavor, ever striving to remake ourselves in our own image. When we have approached true greatness, we have been great not because we were strong but because we were good.

Religion speaks in many voices, some uplifting and some incendiary. With its time-honored capacity to foster peace and its growing potential as an instrument for violence, religion is at once the most elevating and most dangerous power in today's world. The civil religious spirit, too, can promote self-delusion and national arrogance. Or, instructed by the American Creed and thus tapping the deepest sources of our common life, it can vitalize the nation, directing its might to secure our country's integrity. When tuned to the highest anthems of our history, it offers a needful corrective to both relativist and fundamentalist pieties. Healthy expressions of civil religion mitigate the fragmentation of our national ethos, combat the moral attrition endemic to modernism, and secure the foundation of the common good.

The public and private elements of our religious identity as a people tend either to prosper or languish together. The chords of civil religion sound more eloquently when sectarian religious institutions are prophetic and strong. By the same token, when the values taught in churches and temples across the land reflect secular, not spiritual, values, our common faith is diminished.

Vibrant discrete communions and an overarching faith in American ideals are each important, but without fidelity to the latter the national center will not hold. In the midst of our revolution, Benjamin Franklin reminded his fellow signers of the Declaration of Independence, "We must all hang together, or most assuredly we will all hang separately." Franklin's rallying cry epitomizes the pragmatic advantages of *E pluribus unum. Pluribus* alone—the principle of sovereign individualism—endangers the health and vitality of a sovereign people. In our union of faith and freedom, neither alone could be half as redemptive as the two are together.

The evil deeds of our self-appointed enemies must not lull the nation into passive acquiescence to an end-justifies-the-means response. Since American union finds its noblest expression in the devotion we render to liberty, the right to dissent must be preciously guarded. From John Adams's Alien and Sedition Acts to the government's treatment of Japanese Americans in World War II, McCarthyism during the 1950s, and executive branch malpractice (which we now know included torture) justified by 9/11, history suggests that threats to security offer license to overturn fundamental human rights. The government has an obligation to protect public safety, but we must guard against politically convenient yet otherwise unnecessary abridgment of constitutional guarantees. As American historian Arthur M. Schlesinger Jr. reminds us,

> When we talk of the American democratic faith, we must understand it in its true dimensions. It is not an impervious, final, and complacent orthodoxy, intolerant of deviation and dissent, fulfilled in flag salutes, oaths of allegiance, and hands over the heart. It is an ever-evolving philosophy, fulfilling its ideals through debate, self-criticism, protest, disrespect, and irreverence; a tradition in which all have rights of heterodoxy and opportunities for self-assertion. The Creed has been the means by which Americans have haltingly but persistently narrowed the gap between performance and principle. It is what all Americans should learn, because it is what binds all Americans together.

To remain true to its highest values, America must reembody the ideals of democratic pluralism, not rely on the vaunted superiority of modern secular materialism or trust in the persuasive power of military might. Terrorists may hate America as the incarnation of amoral secularism. But this caricature, if justified, is an America watered down. American values go far deeper than untrammeled laissez-faire capitalism and have nothing to do with materialism. They rest on the firm spiritual foundation on which our nation was established.

CHAPTER 7

From Nationalism to Patriotism: Reclaiming the American Creed

In the days leading up to the 2003 invasion of Iraq, precipitated by a national furor over the 9/11 terrorist attacks (in which the nation of Iraq played no role), American patriotism became indistinguishable from nationalistic jingoism. The people at SkyLight Paths chose this moment to publish a book titled Spiritual Perspectives on America's Role as Superpower, *for which I submitted the following essay, a universalist paean to* E pluribus unum *and all that our erstwhile national motto—it was replaced in 1956 by "In God We Trust"—represents. Happily, today, six years later, the recovery of true American patriotism seems under way again.*

The concept of American empire first emerged in the 1890s. Manifest Destiny was its watchword, its staging areas mostly islands and archipelagos from Cuba to the Philippines. Its political architects, principal among them Theodore Roosevelt, John Hay, and Henry Cabot Lodge, were mainstream Christians, if not conspicuously pious men. Nevertheless, American empire had an evangelical subtext from the very beginning. American internationalism commenced, in fact, with American missions. The gun came quickly to hand, but Manifest Destiny led with a prayer book. A band of

Christian evangelists set the tempo for America's march into world history.

Josiah Strong, a young Congregationalist pastor and evangelist, wrote the first manifesto for American internationalism in 1885. An instant best seller, *Our Country: Its Possible Future and Its Present Crisis*, set the moral tone for American expansion. Its popularity led to Strong's appointment as general secretary of the Evangelical Alliance, a leading vehicle for social reform and Christian mission. Strong believed that American Protestantism, ecumenical in spirit and practice, was the perfect catalyst to redeem a divided world. Dedicated to the social gospel, he called for an international crusade to nurture the spirit of liberty, foster peace, and enhance security, all in preparation for the establishment of God's Kingdom. Wedding biblical religion to republican faith, Strong rallied his countrymen to accomplish "the evangelization of the world."

Both as an evangelical Christian and as a social liberal, Strong viewed American expansionism as a spiritual, not a business, imperative. He celebrated the extension of free markets as conduits for Christian and American ideals. Yet, as subsequent American internationalists have also often been, Strong was remarkably parochial. To him, American empire would signal the triumph of Anglo-Saxon values and culture. The net result was white-bread Christian American jingoism. "We are the chosen people," Strong proclaimed. "We cannot afford to wait. The plans of God will not wait. Those plans seem to have brought us to one of the closing stages in the world's career, in which we can no longer drift with safety to our destiny."

Strong's call was answered in two ways: first, by the establishment and rapid growth of an ecumenically sponsored missionary movement; and second, by the extension of military might beyond the nation's borders. Protestant Christianity and American democracy were exported in the same package. To accomplish this, if need be, American values would be supported by American arms.

In retrospect, America's first adventures as a superpower were more than a little ham-fisted. To begin with, the level of ignorance in the White House and State Department about this world we were setting out to redeem was nothing short of remarkable. President

William McKinley's only stated justification for going to war with Spain in 1898 was "to Christianize the Philippines," which happened already to be Christian. By the end of World War I, President Woodrow Wilson had codified an explicit religious mission for the nation's international agenda. Sailing across the Atlantic to take part in the peace conference after the war, Wilson declared, "We are to be an instrument in the hands of God to see that liberty is made secure for mankind." In this conviction, Wilson did not stand alone. Many Christian ministers, including Lyman Abbott, known for his commitment to the social gospel, viewed what turned out to be the first world war as a "twentieth century crusade." That any religious meaning could be wrung out of that conflict demonstrates how quick Americans are to invest their international endeavors with religious portent.

We can learn a lesson from the early collusion of religion in the nation's international agenda. As American empire extended its circle of influence, religious leaders, at the risk of their own integrity, were increasingly tempted to subjugate their theological principles to the interests of American foreign policy. Shortly after the first war ended, to attract converts the Christian Scientists ran a full-page ad in the *New York Times* proclaiming the credo of the denomination's founder, Mary Baker Eddy. The ordering of her beliefs is telling: "I believe strictly in the Monroe Doctrine, in our Constitution, and in the laws of God."

That American policy should be charged with advancing freedom does not constitute a betrayal of either national or religious ideals. Implicit in the overarching faith sponsored by pluralistic democracy is an evangelical charge. If all people are created equal and endowed by their creator with certain inalienable rights, "all people" represents more than merely the people of the United States. American patriotism demands a high level of moral engagement. In this respect, American isolationism is an oxymoron. Today, together with China as the world's only other superpower, how we express our ideals internationally is of utmost importance to people throughout the world.

American nationalism is insufficient to the moral requirements inherent to our fulfillment of this solemn responsibility. There is nothing unique about American nationalism. As with every expression of nationalism, it is grounded in the first law of nature, self-protection. Other countries may benefit from a superpower's nationalistic policies, but their own interests remain secondary. Even the most enlightened nationalism therefore breeds resentment. (It should be remembered that self-defense and not the spread of democracy was the original pretext for our invasion of Iraq.)

Unlike American nationalism, American patriotism *is* unique. As summed up in the Declaration of Independence, this creed is based on other so-called laws of nature, namely liberty and equality. To the extent that the United States betrays its own ideals, American patriotism holds the nation under judgment.

It has done so from the beginning. When established as national writ, "All men are created equal" excluded both women and slaves. The first American feminist manifesto, written by Elizabeth Cady Stanton in 1848, invoked the Declaration of Independence to point out the gap between deed and creed: "We hold these truths to be self-evident; that all men and women are created equal...." In condemning the curse of slavery, Frederick Douglass and Abraham Lincoln did the same. Expressing his dream, the Reverend Dr. Martin Luther King Jr. looked forward to the "day this nation will rise up and live out the true meaning of its creed." From the outset of our history, American patriots have challenged the nation to tune its actions to the key of its ideals.

We fulfill or betray our national destiny dramatically on the international stage. The American ideal of *E pluribus unum* has become an international mandate. Our greatest leaders recognized this half a century ago. President Franklin Delano Roosevelt applied his "four freedoms" (freedom from want and fear, freedom of faith and speech) "everywhere in the world." As chair of the Human Rights Commission of a new United Nations, Eleanor Roosevelt incorporated her husband's four freedoms in the Universal Declaration of Human Rights, a global restatement of America's principles of liberty and justice for all. Adopted by the United Nations General Assembly on December 10, 1948, the Universal Declaration of Human Rights also echoes Jefferson's words in the Declaration of Independence. All people are equally "endowed with reason and conscience." The Preamble declares that "recognition of the inherent dignity and of the equal and inalienable rights of all members of the human family is the foundation of freedom, justice, and peace in the world." By affirming and expanding the founders' vision of "Out of many, one," the United Nations is a monument to American patriotism.

Terrorism is not an American problem, it is a world problem. The battle against terror, not a clash of civilizations but a clash between civilization and anarchy, demands an international front, not a self-appointed savior. American arrogance can only fan the flames American policy is designed to extinguish. One sets a backfire to control a burning forest when the winds are favorable. Otherwise the backfire spreads the very flames that it was intended to quench. Beyond going against the logic of enlightened self-interest, policies that impose an American agenda (simply because American power is sufficient to implement American desire) take a high spiritual toll on the nation itself. From a religious perspective, arrogance expresses pride, and pride is rightly considered the number one sin.

The impulse of American nationalism isolates the United States and turns others against us. It also rescinds the nation's greatest gift. Whether the challenge has been to slow global warming, ban land mines, combat racism, or create an International Criminal Court, we have isolated ourselves from the very councils we are charged, by both power and principle, to lead. At a time when *E pluribus unum*— however idealistic, however difficult to accomplish—is becoming the world's motto, the United States of America, whose founders gave this vision as a gift to the world, too often stands alone.

What a lost opportunity this represents. Following the terrorist attacks in September 2001, people throughout the world expressed unprecedented sympathy for our nation. President Jacques Chirac of France proclaimed, "We are all Americans now." Today [a year later] even America is divided against itself. To have squandered both the world's affection and the united spirit of our citizenry in so brief a span represents a tragic triumph of American nationalism over American patriotism.

During the first chapter of American empire, the mission embarked on by Josiah Strong and other Christian missionaries was well intentioned: to ameliorate social conditions throughout the world and spread the American faith in liberty and justice for all. Our leaders make similar moral claims today. They are one hundred percent half-right. America can and must witness to the higher principles on which this nation is founded. Yet so long as American superpower is indistinguishable from American nationalism writ large, we betray the same moral principles to which we give such self-serving lip service. By so doing, we can only add to the problems we are trying to solve.

Not alone, the most recent chapter of our history reminds us that nationalism can be as blind as love, for it is a form of love. Searching through my grandparents' attic when I was a boy, I found a handsome wooden plaque picturing a soldier in a broad-brimmed American World War I helmet, embossed in burnished copper with the words: "My country, right or wrong." In coining this phrase in 1816 the American naval officer Stephen Decatur (though expressing a preference that his country would turn out to be right, not wrong) proposed the ultimate toast to nationalism. Since responsible power calls itself under judgment, American patriotism refutes this sentiment by emending it more pointedly. Speaking against the extension of Manifest Destiny into the Philippines in 1899, Senator Carl Schurz of Missouri said, "Our country, right or wrong. When right, to be kept right; when wrong, to be put right."

The United States is built on a foundation of belief, not on a foundation of skepticism. By our actions, not our words, this foundation of belief is either justified or betrayed. Patriotic fidelity to the American Creed remains challenging, but it invests the nation with spiritual purpose and, if we honor its precepts, a moral destiny. American nationalism betrays that destiny. What we need today are a few more patriots.

BOOK III

A Liberal Pulpit

CHAPTER 8

The Presidential Pulpit and Religious Politics

Preachers, all preachers, weave their theology into the tapestry of their sermons. My universalist theology found concrete expression from week to week in the All Souls pulpit, which I filled for three decades. The pulpit is not a place to make partisan political pronouncements. Liberal religion, especially in its American incarnation, affirms the separation of church and state, a separation salutary to the independence of each. That said, social issues and government policies often demand that a preacher tackle the great moral issues of the day. Detaching one's faith from matters of public concern privatizes and trivializes it. By the same token, a preacher must speak to the religious questions posed by these great issues, not to the political ones. The church is not a political institution. It stands in judgment on such institutions; it does not and must not serve them. In this section, I include a selection of my sermons on public affairs, not to cover the most important issues we have faced over the last thirty years, but to illustrate how a liberal faith may be applied at times of crisis or national concern. Each reveals how intimately my universalist theology informs my public preaching. To frame the chapters to follow, I open with a sermon on religion and politics preached in early 2003, on the eve of the Iraq invasion.

At times of war, or pending war, almost inevitably we witness a marked increase of religious rhetoric from politicians and political rhetoric from preachers. Critics of this practice base their concern on a variety of grounds. Some argue that the wall of separation between church and state should extend to a complete separation of religion from politics. Jerry Falwell held this position during the civil rights struggle. "Preachers are not called to be politicians but soul winners," Falwell said in 1965, condemning Martin Luther King Jr. and the ministers who marched with him in Selma. In 1972, George McGovern quoted the Bible more often than any presidential candidate since William Jennings Bryan.

Shortly thereafter, Falwell appears to have had a change of heart. In fact, due to the effective way in which he and others on the religious right took a leaf from Dr. King's book and infused their religion with political rhetoric from the mid-1970s onward, more recent critics of the admixture of politics and religion have tended to come from the left, not the right. Antiwar pundits are as acrid in their expressed distaste for President George W. Bush's political piety as were anti–civil rights preachers scornful of the religious politics in the 1960s.

One conclusion we might draw from this does little to flatter the presumption of human consistency. The rule of thumb appears to be, when we agree with a preacher's or president's politics, we have little problem with an admixture of policy and faith; but when we disagree, sensing that there is something dangerous about the admixture, we cry foul.

There is certainly something dangerous about mixing politics and religion. Simply put, whoever invokes God's name may appear or even presume to be wearing God's mantle. This not only trivializes religion by making the Almighty a hireling to human ambition, but also threatens to demonize politics. Abraham Lincoln was the first statesman publicly to admit that mortal enemies pray to the same God for support and guidance and march against one another as God's soldiers, each acting in God's name. After yet another terrible Union defeat, a visitor to the White House told Lincoln that he could nonetheless rest assured that God was on his side. Lincoln blanched. "I can try to be on God's side, Madam, but must not presume that God is on mine." On the other hand, almost every time he condemned slavery, he did so for expressly religious reasons. He introduced "In God We Trust" to the nation's coinage. And, for the first time since John Adams, he employed explicitly Christian language when calling the people to state-sponsored worship (days of thanksgiving and national fasts). At such times Lincoln acted more like an evangelist than the elected leader of a secular government.

If politics and religion form a dangerous mix, they also constitute an inevitable one. To tell a president not to consult his religious beliefs when he acts is to ask him to do something that should be impossible for him to do. By the same token, to ask a minister to disconnect his or her private faith from matters of public moral policy would be to create a spiritual gelding, whose faith, at best, would be inoffensive.

At times in our history, the admixture of religion and politics has elevated the nation's sights. At other times, it has clouded them. For both politician and pastor, the question is not whether religion and politics *should* mix. They *do* mix and will continue to mix. Freedom of religion and freedom of speech almost guarantee that admixture. The question, now as always, is *"How* should they mix?"

President Bush is, with John Quincy Adams, Jimmy Carter, and Woodrow Wilson, one of four confessed and observably pious presidents in this nation's history. To them (but in a wholly different category) might be added Abraham Lincoln, a theologically acute, brooding, and (by the time of the Civil War) deeply devout freethinker. Many of Lincoln's predecessors were resolutely secular. After Lincoln, most of our presidents have held apparently sincere, if unobtrusive, Christian convictions.

Knowing something of a president's beliefs and the sincerity with which he holds them is important for any number of reasons. For one thing, we know then whether or not we should take his religious rhetoric seriously. For instance, given that he wasn't known as a biblical literalist, when Theodore Roosevelt proclaimed at the outset of one political campaign, "We stand at Armageddon and battle for the Lord," no one, fortunately, was tempted to take him literally. On the other end of the presidential religious spectrum, Jimmy Carter, a born-again Baptist, ever careful not to impose his faith on the people he was elected to represent, almost completely eschewed biblical rhetoric in his pronouncements.

Whether religious or not, all of our presidents have invoked the name "God" at times of crisis. To invoke God's name (the usual presidential device) is not in and of itself to claim God's authority. For instance, when Franklin Delano Roosevelt closed his declaration at the outset of our entry into World War II with the words "so help us God," his was a prayer of petition, not a theological boast. With only one exception that I know of—he predicted Allied victory by declaring it God's will—FDR's theological language is never arrogant or presumptive. When he employed God language he did so to challenge the American people to sacrifice for a noble cause or rise up and live according to their highest values.

It should perhaps not surprise us that the three presidents who invoked God's name most often in their addresses were all wartime presidents: Lincoln, Wilson, and Roosevelt. I'm not speaking here of the formulaic "God bless you and God bless the United States of America" that Lyndon Johnson introduced and Ronald Reagan standardized for all future presidents' use. In their proclamations and even in general conversation, Lincoln and Wilson in particular went on at great length concerning the relationship between American policy and the workings of the Almighty. Lincoln always spoke of God and God's will with deep humility, Wilson with what might strike an outsider as insufferable arrogance. I'll offer but a single example: "The stage is set," Wilson once proclaimed. "The destiny is disclosed. It has come about by no plan of our conceiving, but by the hand of God who led us into this way. We cannot turn back. We can only go forward, with lifted eyes and freshened spirit, to follow the vision.... America shall in truth show the way. The light streams on the path ahead, and nowhere else."

Wilson saw the United States as God's instrument to redeem a fallen world. "With malice toward none, with charity toward all," Lincoln recognized himself among the fallen. Franklin Roosevelt took a middle course between the two. He drew his religious script explicitly from the founders' vision, speaking of liberty and equality as God's gifts to all, and pledging our nation to defend freedom "everywhere in the world."

Where then does President George W. Bush fall on this spectrum? Many political and religious commentators who oppose President Bush's new military doctrine of preemptive deterrence at the same time condemn his ever more extensive recourse to religious language and statements of faith in his speeches. All I can tell you is that Bush's religious rhetoric is closer to Roosevelt's than it is, say, to Wilson's. When he said in his State of the Union address that "the liberty we prize is not America's gift to the world, it is God's gift to humanity," Bush was paraphrasing the Declaration of Independence, written by a skeptical unitarian, Thomas Jefferson.

Which brings me to political preaching. As with religious politics, in general how those in the pew receive their preacher's pronouncements from the pulpit pivots on whether or not they agree with his or her political stands. Even as I would not presume to censor a president's sincere expressions of faith, however, I also would not censor a minister's voice on public policy. Our lives and thoughts simply do not compartmentalize that easily. Where I do draw the line, with both presidents and pastors, is at the point of presumption—preaching from on high, wrapping one's rhetoric in God's mantle, telling people what political positions they must hold if they are to be considered good Americans or good Christians or even good Unitarian Universalists. Here Abraham Lincoln has much to teach all of us. We see through a glass darkly. Our knowledge is imperfect. We cannot predict the future. And we are all sinners.

The Bible is chock-full of political, prophetic, edgy preaching from beginning to end. Certainly our own liberal religious tradition is built on a history of "public ministry." We are saved in the world and for the world, not from the world. In fact, what is true for ministers is true for all of us. Unitarian ethicist James Luther Adams speaks of the priesthood and prophethood of all believers. There is no presumption of orthodoxy here, either religious or political, only of individual responsibility. As Unitarian Universalists, we celebrate and defend freedom of thought. We facilitate the action of like-minded souls, while at the same time opening our doors to many currents of opinion, remembering that popular opinion often turns out to have been wrong even as opinion initially held by a courageous voice or two may later be proved right.

Our overarching purpose within these walls is religious—not social, not cultural, not political. There are so many places where political views can be expressed unfettered by religious concerns. This congregation is not such a place. Everything we do here is guided and ennobled, to the degree we can submit to its yoke, by religious concern.

Whatever authority your ministers have—and you give it to us, we do not claim it as our own—is religious authority. It is spiritual authority. Speaking for myself, however, when I read the Bible or say my prayers I can't help but ponder what is happening in the world today. Whatever arrests my most reverent attention becomes a dimension of my office. I preach from where I am to where I think you are, but this has nothing to do with our respective opinions. It has to do with entering and advancing the conversation that goes on at times like these at the dinner table and over the watercooler, in our dreams and deep within our souls. With so many others, I am shaken to my very bones by the threat posed by terrorism and the threat posed by preemptive war. That is what I must and shall continue to preach about.

About Jonah, for instance, after he was saved. After Jonah was saved, he became God's most loyal lieutenant. God sent him to pronounce judgment on the city of Nineveh for all its transgressions. Then God changed his mind. God did, not Jonah. Jonah would rather die than see Nineveh go unpunished. Here history and tragedy threaten to become one and the same. God says to Jonah, "I took mercy on you. Why should I not take mercy on the people of Nineveh, one hundred thousand strong and cattle without number?" An emphatic universalist moment in the Bible, here is Yahweh, the God of the Jews, saving the people of Nineveh, themselves not Jews. Not to mention saving his enemy from his very own prophet. One day soon, I must preach to you on Jonah.

And on Abraham. I must preach on Abraham again. When Abraham takes Isaac up to slay him on the rock (Isaac, his very son, to be

slain at God's command), I ask myself, "Could Abraham even possibly have been listening? Did he really hear God right: 'Go and slay
your firstborn son'? Is that really what God wanted Abraham to do?"
And then I read with wonder, always with wonder, when the ram
jumps from the brush and God offers the ram to take the place of
Abraham's son.

Imagine if Abraham had been as dutiful as Jonah. Imagine Abraham (the father of Israel, the father of Christianity, the father of
Islam) so fixated on following God's instructions that he doesn't even
notice the ram. In the name of God, he kills his own son. Consider
how many of Abraham and Isaac's children have in fact forgotten this
story from their scriptures and done precisely that.

Abraham's progeny and Jonah. God's loyal servants. Acting in
God's name. Getting the message wrong. We don't mean to. Really
we don't. But so often, we—parents, presidents, and pastors alike—get
the message wrong. We get it wrong and history becomes tragedy.

And so I go down by the bank of my sorrow, of our sorrow. I go
down by the bank to pray. I pray for our president. I pray for all the
Jonahs, blinded by self-righteous anger. I pray for all Abraham's dutiful progeny, generation upon generation, preparing their own children for slaughter. I pray for all the latter-day Isaacs, splayed once
again on desert rocks. I pray for the gift of a ram.

CHAPTER 9

The Commonwealth of God

*Plato tells the story of a charioteer and his two fiery steeds, warring passions that threaten to run away with his life should he pay them insufficient heed. In 1987, keynoting a Princeton University ecumenical peace conference (sponsored by the Nuclear Disarmament Fund of the Coalition for Nuclear Disarmament), I reinterpreted this parable to depict the danger of nuclear annihilation through accident or neglect. From well before its date of delivery to today, this danger presents the world's greatest and most stubbornly ignored peril. Inspired in part by the book I was writing then (*The Seven Deadly Virtues*), I had this to say on the dangers of nuclear proliferation and on what we might do to address these dangers—become citizens in the Commonwealth of God.*

I wonder if this is how the world will end. On one side, maybe ours, a computer error. Scrambled signals in the data feed. Orders misdirected. Backup computers fail. Who knows what might happen to pull us off course without our knowing it? After all, our crews are highly trained, our systems the best. As far as anyone can tell, everything's in order, except, perhaps, the communications system. For some odd reason, those in charge, some second-level commander and his crew, can't seem to communicate with anyone. Nothing much to worry

64

about though. They tinker a bit, chatting among themselves about the folks back home. I wonder. Could the beginning of the end of the world be anything like this? A computer failure? An innocent mistake?

On the other side of the world, an alarm sounds. Something is amiss. Systems are readied and placed on full alert. Interceptors are sent out. Those in charge, some second-level commander and his crew, try to communicate with us, but only briefly, and their attempts at communication fail. They perceive intent instead of error in our actions, mistaking us for something we are not. Or perhaps they simply go by the book: act first and ask questions later, just as they have been instructed to do. A deadly mistake. They open fire.

And what about the rest of us, passengers, traveling on a voyage through space, friend and foe alike, Christian, Muslim, Hindu, Jew, black and white, Communist and capitalist, traveling in enforced togetherness toward a common destiny? We are flying through the night. The shades are drawn, the lights low. One woman gently rocks her baby; another puts the final touches on a major article that she hopes may revolutionize her field. Some of us are drinking, some conversing quietly with friends. One young man plays solitaire, another studies for his exams. Many are tucked in for the evening, wrapped in blankets, fitfully dreaming or sleeping soundly.

Or are we all nodding, half-asleep to the dangers that, without warning, threaten to terminate the fragile experiment of life on this planet?

It is hard to imagine as we make our plans for tomorrow. And love our children. And hate our enemies. And build up our arsenals, both personal and national, to defend ourselves against them. It is hard to imagine as we doze off with our tickets in our pockets. First an innocent mistake, then a deadly mistake. And no one left to report that the target has been destroyed.

You may recognize the scene: the downing of Korean Air Lines Flight 007 by Soviet jets over the Sea of Japan in 1983. There is only one difference. Confusion, countercharges, and denials would not follow the destruction of the earth in a nuclear holocaust.

Nothing would.

Plato tells the story of a charioteer and his two fiery steeds. One day when driving, the charioteer grows drowsy and drifts off to sleep. No longer feeling the restraint of the reins, his steeds bolt from their path, leading both themselves and their driver in uncontrolled flight toward an abyss. In this story, the driver is drawn into danger unconscious of his peril. But as the chariot lurches toward the pit, a distant bystander, perceiving the danger, issues an alarm. In a ringing voice, he shouts out to the charioteer, "Wake up! Save yourself!" The startled driver awakens, perceives his peril, draws in his steeds, and saves himself from certain destruction.

Plato interprets this parable in terms of self-discipline. The steeds are intended to represent animal desires, lusts, and passions, which, when uncontrolled, can dominate our individual lives and even destroy them. The driver is the understanding, the intelligence, the wisdom with which we are endowed, that we might tame our desires and have dominion over our impulses.

But there is a modern way to read this parable. From the standpoint of relationship rather than self-knowledge, salvation becomes a community-wide, not an individual, effort. It has communal as well as individual consequences. By such a reading, the key moment in this story comes when a distant bystander bestirs himself and issues a call of alarm.

Adapted to contemporary realities, we might reinterpret Plato's parable as follows.

This is a nuclear chariot. The two steeds represent the classical virtues of hope and fortitude, to which the driver has given increasingly loose rein. Our hope lies in the continuing power of deterrence. Our fortitude rests in the will never to stint in amassing armaments to protect ourselves from, even ultimately to vanquish, an evil, godless adversary. These arguments have been offered up so often, and with such persuasive passion, that the driver of this deadly cargo has been lulled asleep. Thus, when the distant bystander cries out, not only is he protecting the charioteer from self-destruction, he is also protecting himself and his neighbors from being immolated when this chariot, a potential fireball of unprecedented proportion, careens into the abyss toward which it is hurtling.

Whatever your politics, if you doubt the importance of the forthcoming Intermediate-Range Nuclear Forces Treaty, think of it and its supporters as distant bystanders, calling our chariot back home.

In Plato's reading, an individual is saved from his personal passions, which we later called sins. Today, what threatens the survival of one individual endangers us all—not our sins so much as our "virtues," our ideological passions, things in which we have absolute faith, ensured by hope and defended by fortitude. We employ these virtues to legitimate our power, sharpen our competitive edge, establish criteria of superiority, and defend otherwise indefensible actions. In an age in which survival itself hinges on the development of an alternative set of relational values, the old virtues, if practiced in the old ways, are deadly.

Near the end of his term in office Richard D. Lamm of Colorado, who had earned the sobriquet Governor Gloom for his unsentimental journeys into the future, began one of his speeches with the following popular parable. The U.S. fleet is on the high seas. Suddenly a blip appears on the radar screen. "Tell that ship to change its course fifteen degrees," barks the admiral. The radioman complies, only to be signaled back, "You change your course fifteen degrees." Incensed, the admiral gets on the radio himself. "I am an admiral in the U.S. Navy. Change your course fifteen degrees at once." The word comes back: "You change your course fifteen degrees. I am a lighthouse."

Summing up what he had learned during twelve years as governor, Lamm draws this moral: "Beware of solutions appropriate to the past but disastrous to the future." Or, as the old hymn reminds us: "New occasions teach new duties, time makes ancient good uncouth."

If the nuclear arms race offers the ultimate specter of competing virtues triggering potentially deadly consequences, many other specters loom on our horizon. In an age of interdependence, the old virtues, in fact any virtue possessed as an attainment rather than shared as a community good, directly threaten our shared future. In an interdependent age, the question is not "What can I do to be saved?" but "What can we do to save one another?" Whenever our possession of something (even justice, faith, love, and truth) denies others access to it (selective justice, militant faith, exclusive love, dogmatic truth) we become traitors, subverting the Commonwealth of God.

Members in the Commonwealth of God are not bound together by the specifics of their religion, for the nature of our interdependency does not require this. Rather we are bound by the shared recognition that when one person suffers, all suffer; when we violate one life, all lives are violated; when we pollute the earth, all living things are stained; when one nation threatens the security of another, it, too, becomes less secure; when we place the planet in mortal danger, we hazard the future of our own children as well as the children of our enemies.

Competitive virtues elevate winners by diminishing losers. This is especially hazardous in competition between countries. In the age of the global village and the global economy, while the balance may be tipped temporarily in one side's favor, if sustained such imbalances set up the possibility of a tidal wave of terrifying proportion, which may start all the way on the other side of the world and end up crashing down on our own shores.

Given human nature and history, to propose a relational, cooperative, and fraternal, or kinship-based, ethic fashioned to strengthen the interdependent web of being may seem idealistic and naive. In fact, it is desperately realistic. Interrelatedness is not simply a theological concept; it is a new truth.

We are made insecure by others' insecurity. This is the new truth, though many old prophets have spoken it. All of us are part of one body, even those who never awaken to the nature of our interdependencies. We may spend our lives as anti-bodies within the body of Christ (or atman or God or the universe), but still, whatever sustenance we may garner springs from this common source. When we squander our lives we squander life itself; when we give our lives away we enhance all life, including our own.

Religious or otherwise, every war between peoples, parties, or faiths is a civil war, brothers and sisters killing one another with words or weapons, renting the one fabric, riving the body of God. This is why we need new metaphors to illustrate the interdependent nature of all life, images that will awaken us to our kinship with one another, allowing for distinctive beliefs, while offering a canopy underneath which all beliefs, howsoever disparate, may reside. The Kingdom of God must become a Commonwealth.

Reducing all beliefs to a lowest common denominator will not work, nor would it be worthy if it did. Bleeding religions of their particularity would boil out their nutrients. Each faith has its particular strength, drawn from history and prophecy, from shared reflection on life's meaning to common patterns of worship that together invest its symbols and message with saving power. Because of this, every religion sponsors values different from every other, in some cases strikingly so. Anyone who talks glibly of one religion for all people has little religion to begin with.

The Commonwealth of God is grounded not in uniformity but mutuality. We are not replicates of one another but related to one another in a single body with many different members, each with a unique gift.

Today, for better and for worse, we humans are both more knowledgeable and more powerful. "Here on earth God's work must truly be our own," John Kennedy said in his inaugural address. From cloning to nuclear holocaust, we hold Genesis and Armageddon in our hands. With our knowledge continuing to outstrip our wisdom, whether we can begin to handle God's work remains doubtful. But if not, there will be hell to pay, since the punishment for hubris, best defined as an arrogation of powers belonging to the gods by human beings who have no natural right to them, is nemesis, utter and terrible destruction. The earth, like Flight 007 or Plato's chariot before the driver was awakened to his own and our shared peril, would burst into flame and be extinguished. This horrific, tragic outcome need not and must not come to pass.

If, in the first chapter of Genesis, humankind was created in the image of God and given dominion over the earth, charged to fill the earth and to subdue it, in the second chapter, which reflects a different strand of the ancient traditions brought together in the Bible, we are placed here not to subdue the earth, but "to dress and to keep it." As passenger and pilot, bystander and charioteer, it is this we must remember as we fly together through space on this hospitable planet, whose fate we hold in our trembling hands.

CHAPTER 10

Fear and Terror

The bombing of the Federal Building in Oklahoma City on April 19, 1995, brought home to Americans the threat of terrorism in this country. Although angered by the bombing of the World Trade Center in New York City in 1993 and confused by the deadly confrontation between federal government agents and the Branch Davidian religious sect near Waco, Texas, that same year, the bombing of a government building in the middle of the country resulting in 168 deaths and injuries to many others rocked public assumptions. That such an event could occur in the "heartland of America"—as almost every newspaper and television news show reported in shock—convinced many Americans that terrorism was no longer an activity confined to the Middle East and Europe. The immediate reaction was that agents of a foreign government or a radical religious group must have been responsible for committing this terrible deed. To my shame, I shared this reaction, although the bombing was soon discovered to have been the work of two U.S. Army veterans who shared a violent hatred with the federal government. The bombing, just after Easter, prompted me to abandon my planned sermon the following Sunday in order to discuss my own reactions to the event and to warn against the dangers of ethnic and religious stereotyping.

How distant Easter seems. Only a week ago we gathered in this peaceful sanctuary to trumpet the victory of love over death. One week later we are left to sort through the rubble and carnage that litter the once quiet streets of Oklahoma City, our hearts possessed with grief, anger, and fear. It's as if Easter this year has been turned on its head, the holy calendar reversed, resurrection first and then, three days later, the crucifixion.

Obviously whatever I had planned to speak about this morning is of no consequence in light of the week's events. In a single blast, the world we live in is dramatically changed.

The question remains, how do we sort through the rubble and carnage? How can we extricate some meaning or guidance from this terrible tragedy? I am as off balance as you are. Having been transfixed by the television reports, I now want to run from them, from the images of horror, from the tears and the anger. I am looking for a good movie, even a bad movie, anything to take me away. And I will find one. But I also know that I must look deeper and further, both into myself and into the life we share as citizens of this country, even of the world.

I must look deeper into myself, in part because my initial response to the Oklahoma City bombing was to fix my attention and fear on a composite, stereotypical image of a Muslim terrorist: bearded, wiry, dark-eyed, alien, inscrutable, fanatical, terrifying. Even after I saw the composite drawings of the two suspects, I thought to myself, "Well, the one could be Arab. Perhaps the other is a bad rendering. After all, they caught that man on his way from Oklahoma City to Jordan, his bags filled with bomb-making material and photographs of American military sites."

His name was Ibrahim Ahmad. They held him for sixteen hours. He was very cooperative. His bags were not filled with bomb-making material and photographs of American military sites. Nor did the other suspects I read about, Asad and Anis Siddiqy, have anything to do with the bombing. They were Queens taxi drivers working on an immigration problem. They lived with Mohammed Chafti. He, too, was grilled for fifteen hours. I understand that. All leads had to be scrupulously followed. But I also know that if I were given a multiple-choice terrorist quiz two days ago, and asked to guess between Asad Siddiqy, Mohammed Chafti, Ibrahim Ahmad, Timothy McVeigh, and Terry Nichols, I would have failed the test.

The threat of internationally sponsored murder and mayhem by such groups as Hamas and Hezbollah is very real. An old friend of mine, Steve Emerson, author of the now-famous documentary *Jihad in America*, presents the evidence in convincing detail. But I also know, or should know, that no people, no faith, have a corner on hatred. Take the woman who said of our Muslim neighbors on a talk show this week, "No wonder this happened. These countries, their culture, have no respect for human life." Or the caller who threatened to blow up a discount variety store on Fifth Avenue owned by a Syrian-born citizen. "We're going to get you and we're going to get your family." "This is not a question of anybody's country of origin," President Clinton reminds us. "This is not a question of anybody's religion. This was murder, this was evil, this was wrong. Human beings everywhere, all over the world, will condemn this out of their own religious convictions."

So I am troubled, deeply troubled, by my knee-jerk reaction.

All of us are prejudiced. But when thoughtful people do not work hard to temper their prejudices, bigots—those who celebrate prejudice—will only be vested with more power. Bigots like Timothy McVeigh and Terry Nichols.

I've noticed that a favorite question posed by reporters to people on the street is some variation of, "Does it bother you that Americans are responsible for this?" "It devastates me," one woman replied. "I just can't believe that an American, that a human being, could do this." There are millions of Arab Americans, millions of Muslim Americans—Muslim American human beings. They are only as likely to buy the hatred spewed by Hamas or Hezbollah as are white-bread Midwestern Christian Americans likely to feed on the equally bigoted and dangerous paranoia fostered by groups like the Michigan Militia, led by Norman Olson, self-styled "pistol-packin' preacher" and gun-store owner. Or the Arizona Patriots, whose members believe that the United States is being run by the Protocols of Zion and about to be conquered by the United Nations.

Friday's *New York Post* [April 23, 1995] ran a cartoon of three Muslims laughing and burning an American flag at the base of the Statue of Liberty, which read, "Give us your tired, your poor, your huddled masses; your terrorists, your murderers, your slime, your evil cowards, your religious fanatics, your welfare cheats." I can think of at least two flag-waving Christians wedded to their own perverse reading of the Bill of Rights who would have laughed knowingly at that cartoon. Believing that our government has fallen prey to foreigners, welfare cheats, and slime, among whom they numbered blacks and Jews, and obsessed with their guns, these two unimaginably sick Americans are responsible for the deaths of nearly two hundred innocent people, victims of the same kind of hate that such a cartoon unwittingly fosters.

Timothy McVeigh, a "quiet, shy churchgoing youth from upstate New York, who liked computers, basketball, and cars." Terry Nichols, a "good neighbor," with a bumper sticker on his car that boasted the words, "American and Proud." The former, arrested carrying a licensed Glock semiautomatic pistol, loaded with hollow-point bullets, known as cop-killers, slept with his guns. The latter is known to have experimented with making fertilizer bombs in his barn.

Tom Metzger, head of something called the White Aryan Resistance, said yesterday: "I have told people for years, at least since 1984, when The Order declared war on the central government of the United States, that the government of this country—what we call the criminals—had better start listening to the dispossessed white people, the dispossessed majority. There was a hot war in the 1980s, and since then there's been a cold war, and now things are heating up again."

We don't need to look outside our borders or to another faith to discover our common enemy. He also lurks within, inspired not by the Koran but by the book of Revelation, his hatred of the government fed by the incendiary, divisive antigovernment rhetoric employed so successfully by certain of our political leaders, his fears fomented into paranoia and then violence by the American gun lobby.

We don't have to look any further than *The Turner Diaries*, a hateful, frightening book deemed the bible of the survivalist movement. Positing the secret takeover of the government by Jews seeking to strip good Americans of their guns in an attempt to establish a new world order, the book begins with these words: "Today, it finally began. After all those years of talking—and nothing but talking—we have finally taken our first action. We are at war with the system, and it is no longer a war of words." In this book, extremists blow up a federal office building at nine fifteen in the morning. The narrative continues: "Our worries about the relatively small size of the bomb were unfounded; the damage is immense. The scene in the courtyard was one of utter devastation. Overturned trucks and automobiles, smashed office furniture and building rubble were strewn wildly about—and so were the bodies of a shockingly large number of victims. They have clearly made the decision to portray the bombing of the FBI building as the atrocity of the century. All the bombings, arsons and assassinations carried out by the Left in this country have been rather small time in comparison."

And so we come to April 19. The day that American patriots defended Lexington and Concord against the Redcoats in 1775. The day that survivalist Randy Weaver, holed up in Ruby Ridge, Idaho, was informed by compatriots of a government plot against him in 1992. The day that the Branch Davidians immolated themselves in 1993. And the day that white supremacist Richard Snell, who murdered a black police officer and a Jewish businessman, was to be executed in Arkansas in 1995. That was last Wednesday. With this date as a mantra, one right-wing newsletter, the *Montana Militia*, warned that Snell would die, "unless we act now!!!" Snell, a murderer, did die. So did scores of innocents in Oklahoma City. Two centuries after the first Minutemen bravely fought at the Lexington bridge, two centuries after our founders, mindful of events leading up to the shot heard round the world, passed the Second Amendment to our nation's Constitution establishing our right to a citizens' militia, a far deadlier blast in Oklahoma City has been heard round the world, and history itself, our own nation's history, lies twisted in the wreckage.

There will be great pressure in the days ahead to enact an Omnibus Counterterrorism Act to protect us from Muslim fanatics. I wish only that certain of the most vociferous proponents of this legislation would examine their own consciences to ponder how their support for lifting a ban on semiautomatic weapons actually enhances the opportunity for terrorism to occur in this country. I hope they will hear their own words about protecting our sacred right to buy and keep arms echo back from the writings and voices of the hate mongers actually responsible for the tragedy in Oklahoma City. I hope they will think, at least a little, about how the seeds of division grow, how rhetoric that plays on our fears of one another, on our differences, the rhetoric that scapegoats, that pits neighbor against neighbor, can so easily blossom into full-blown bigotry, and with such devastating consequence.

When we answer hatred with hate and fire with fire, we do not lessen but only compound the object of our enmity. Fighting delinquency by becoming delinquents (sending federal agents to storm their Idaho shack, killing his wife and child in the crossfire), we do not destroy the Randy Weavers of this world. We do not extirpate the power expressed in David Koresh's paranoia and fascination with violence by killing four of his followers and then embargoing his compound until he and his sect immolate themselves. We do nothing to diminish the white supremacism and anti-Semitism spewed by Richard Snell when we execute him for his heinous crimes. As the tragedy in Oklahoma City reminds us, violence begets more violence. Even the most just violence, whether institutional or accidental, contributes to the climate of fear and hatred, which spawns yet more violence in an unending spiral.

If we have learned anything, we should have learned this from the endless succession of terrorist activity in the Middle East. Now we can study it on our own soil. If I were asked yesterday whether the perpetrators of this evil act should receive the death penalty, I might have been tempted to say "perhaps," betraying my own principles. Today, I say no. I couldn't bear for them to become martyrs for the next wave of Timothy McVeighs and Terry Nicholses. Let the blood be on their hands, not ours.

I expect that we will execute them. When we do, even as I have wrestled this week with my own prejudice against Arab Americans, I will again, I am sure, wrestle against my primitive, all-too-human desire for vengeance. Not my finest part, but part of me will cheer when these brutal men die. I am ashamed of that, but it is so.

I will be far more ashamed if I do not dedicate a greater part of my energy to combating—and that is not too strong a word—the climate of violence that is poisoning this country. Begin with guns. Ban more. Restrict others. Enforce and enhance licensing procedures. Make guns difficult to buy. Ban semiautomatic weapons. And enact severe penalties for illegal sale or possession.

I will also be ashamed if I do not do everything in my small power to reclaim the history and symbols of this great nation from the anti-American, anti-Christian white supremacist and survivalist zealots who have turned the courageous Minutemen of Concord and the American Bill of Rights into fertilizer for their bombs. As far as it lies in our power, and while admitting some necessary abridgment forced by prudence, we must not permit ourselves to be held hostage by our fears, driven to compromise precious American rights far more essential to the survival of this republic than the right to bear arms. The only way to do this is to answer fear, the fear these zealots and their unwitting political champions foment so successfully, with greater faith, the faith of our founders, a faith in one nation, indivisible, with liberty and justice for all. We must answer in the spirit of the people of Oklahoma City, whose courage, bravery, self-sacrifice, and neighborly love remind us once again of what it really means to be a true American. We must answer according to the best that is within the human heart, not imitate the worst.

Perhaps the best way to counter fear with faith is to begin with our own prejudices. These we can do something about, something more than a gesture. Tomorrow I shall call a Muslim cleric and invite him to preach at All Souls as soon as possible. This afternoon, at the Adult Education Committee meeting, I will urge that we devote a month next fall to the study of Islam. Most of us are profoundly ignorant about the teachings of Islam, an ignorance that feeds our prejudice.

In the meantime, mindful of life's fragility, let us remember how fortunate we are. Please, treat one another with kindness. Be thankful for the days we are given. There is time for us; there is still time, time to love and also time to learn.

CHAPTER 11

Shall We Overcome?

In 1993, for the first time since Congress established it as a federal holiday, all fifty states celebrated Martin Luther King Day. Across the country, ceremonies were held honoring Dr. King, who, if he had not been slain on April 4, 1968, would have been sixty-four years old on January 18, 1993. Fifteen years later, on what would have been the week of Dr. King's seventy-ninth birthday, Barack Obama was sworn in as president of the United States, answering the question I pose in the title of this sermon with a much less qualified yes.

Holidays exist for two reasons. The first might be called the "gathering" or "significant cause." We take time off to ponder something essential or meaningful in the lives we share. All religious and national holidays spring from some deep collective need to ponder or celebrate, to mourn or give thanks. They exist as compass points for our souls.

But they exist for another reason as well. Even those who participate in the religious or patriotic ceremonies that mark these holidays tend to lapse into a primary appreciation of their secondary cause, vacation. The long weekend, the gift of a little discretionary time, closed schools, the luxury of an extra day off. We need that too. We need occasions that break the tyranny of a daily grind. We need to vacate, to relax. In and of itself that is a good thing.

But because it is a good thing, we can easily overlook the reason we have been given this time. We can overlook what it was that caused our forebears to establish a holiday in the first place. Veterans Day, Labor Day, and Presidents' Day have become basically interchangeable national holidays almost completely stripped of their essential or original meaning. They are plain vanilla, all-American three-day weekends. We look forward to them not in anticipation of honoring those who have served our country in war, died for our country, participated in the union movement, or whatever. We look forward to them because we get a Monday off.

Not all of us get tomorrow off. That is probably not a bad thing, because, so far anyway, the newest of our national holidays is, for many of us, still more a day *on* than a day *off*. It hasn't been homogenized or pasteurized into a generic celebration. And, for better or worse, it won't be for some time, because what it celebrates has yet to come to pass.

More than any other, Martin Luther King Day is the quintessential American patriotic holiday. Through the pain of its true sponsors, it harks back to the aspirations of our founders and passions of our prophets. It permits us no easy celebrations, no mindless, instantly forgotten rituals, because, the moment we pay attention, it reminds us that we have yet to overcome our own prejudices and fears. If we are paying any attention at all, it reminds us of just how far we have to go to break down the many barriers between people that subvert the idealistic blueprint for this republic, "Out of many, one."

For a liberal preacher this should have been an easy sermon to write, but it wasn't. The reason it wasn't is that I am more aware than ever that my own life experience is so radically different than that of any person of color in this country that for me to wax eloquent on the evils of racism would be a benign but basically hollow exercise. I know little, firsthand, about the evils of racism. Three hours in a movie theater watching Spike Lee's *Malcolm X* proved that point. I could and did sympathize profoundly, but to empathize, to get in someone else's skin and feel what they feel, is a different matter entirely. The most important thing I learned while watching that movie is how enormous the gap is between my own experience of growing up and that of almost every African American person or member of any other ethnic or religious minority in our society.

Let me tell you a little about the two sermons I wrote this week that you are not going to hear this morning. The first you would have liked. It was about the importance of continuing our efforts to cross Ninety-sixth Street, to work with our sister congregation and our adopted school, to enhance our work with the Children's Task Force, the AIDS Task Force, our soup kitchens and homeless scout troops, to build up our service programs by offering more help to our neighbors. All of this activity (not an option for us planted so comfortably on Manhattan's gold coast, but an ethical mandate) fulfills Martin Luther King Jr.'s social gospel. It was an unobjectionable, very boring sermon, and I canned it.

The second sermon you would not have liked. It pointed out that we are a basically rich Upper East Side congregation of unselfconscious racists who think far more highly than we ought to of ourselves.

The third sermon, which, awkward though it may be, you are now hearing, is poised somewhere uncomfortably between the first two. We are doing good things in this church. But for the great majority of us—not others, but us—to benefit fully from these things, we must examine ourselves and our own inheritance of privilege more closely.

Robert Coles has written several books about children, rich and poor, black and white. One of the books he wrote was about me and most of us here this morning. As a child of social privilege, not wealth, but privilege—my father, a comfortable product of the middle class, was nonetheless the poorest U.S. senator—I grew up with what Coles calls a "sense of entitlement." I assumed that I could do anything, be anything. In contrast, for so many others in our society, entitlement and privilege can only be won at tremendous cost, and even when won, remain precarious.

Think about it this way. What would it feel like to be unwanted? An unwanted child, an unwanted neighbor, an unwanted race. A problem for society. A burden. A price tag. Your fate to be carved on the public plate, every social program a piece of meat offered by do-good liberals and pulled away by financially responsible conservatives. And then, when the pain becomes too great, when you speak out or act out, you are branded as ungrateful or counterproductive. How do you get it right? How do you contribute and excel if you start out life as a problem?

My great-grandmother, who grew up in Idaho with Native Americans as neighbors, was fond of quoting the old saw that we cannot know another's pain unless we walk a mile in his or her moccasins. How does a child of entitlement fit his or her feet into the shoes of a child of unentitlement? What we usually do is tell them to work hard in school, avoid drugs, do all the things that we ourselves did successfully, at least part of the time, without ever having to think about ourselves as problem cases. Yet for someone who has wants and needs just like us, but is born unwanted, it's completely different. Until we can begin to understand how different it is, we just won't get it.

I don't care how liberal you are. The problem is that we children of entitlement (and nine out of ten of us here this morning fit the bill) can help ease the pain of the unentitled far more easily than we can feel their pain. As long as this remains the case, those we help are as likely to turn their backs on us as they are to thank us. And then we, feeling hurt, may well turn on them. Resist the temptation. There is nothing noble about people of privilege feeling sorry for themselves for being misunderstood.

So how shall we break the lock? I have only one idea, and I am not sure how often it will work. Step back and recall how you act and feel when you are, or sense you are, unwanted. It happens to each of us, probably every day. We enter a room and it feels like the wrong room; everyone else seems at home; we don't know what to do, or even how to get out without some painful encounter. Or we have been rejected or ignored by someone whose help we need or opinion we value. Every child of privilege is also at times an unwanted child. We know that and we feel it. We just don't think of ourselves that way.

By the same token, every unwanted child can gain, through far harder work than most of us could easily imagine, a sense of entitlement. That is one thing about this country. It can be done. But for it to happen in anything like an evenhanded way, more than a few pairs of moccasins will have to be exchanged. Somehow, the unwanted child in each of us will have to find a way to reach out to other unwanted children, make a real connection, and find that this connection constitutes the greatest privilege of all, communion, friendship, compassion, even love.

Capturing the difficulty we face in celebrating this holiday, perhaps the most important speech delivered this week was by a seventeen-year-old black student at Horace Mann School. "Dr. King's dream has not come true for me," said student body president Sheldon Golber, according to a report in the *Daily News*. "There is no symphony of brotherhood in America. Everything is messed up."

His eyes glistened as he recalled a visit to Italy, when he was the first black person to visit a rural mountain village and the people accepted him. He took a little black rock home with him, calling it a stone of hope.

"Now what do I do with it?" he asked. "Do I use it like my Palestinian brothers in the West Bank, or my African brothers in the streets of Johannesburg? Or will it be used against me as I am chased from the streets of Bensonhurst?"

Again we are reminded that there is no easy way out, no easy way to build the bridge to Martin Luther King Jr.'s dream. Yet his dream is simple. It is predicated on the fact that we are all human, flawed and filled with promise. Whether children of entitlement or unentitlement, we are all children of God.

How do we realize this? How do we, Universalists in name, become universalists in fact? Perhaps if we can draw from our own limited experience of being problem children, unwanted, in the way, out of place. Perhaps if we can store it in our memory and bring it out when children who are really without privilege struggle in our midst for respect or hope or love, we will begin to see our own tears shining in their eyes.

How much better this, how much more helpful than drawing from our strengths—not the weaknesses we share but the strengths that come more easily—to offer our support. The support we offer is good, not bad. I know that. But it fails to provide the one thing most needful, for us and for those we seek to help: recognizing that we are truly one, one people who know how to suffer and can identify with others to help them emerge from their own pain.

This may sound a little sentimental, a little pious: to draw from our weakness to help tap another's strength. Perhaps it is. But it is also biblical. To empty ourselves and be filled. To lose ourselves and be found. It is Gospel. The Good News.

One more piece of good news. This is a new holiday we are celebrating. We still have time to begin to get it right.

CHAPTER 12

World Peace 2000

Leading up to the millennium, the fully plugged-in world whirled in a dither. When the clocks ticked from one century to another, would our computers send us back a century, leading to a massive breakdown, paralyzing the brave new world? The hour passed without incident. But the wild fear provoked by Y2K (that everything would fall apart) testified so eloquently to the interconnected, interdependent new world we now share that I chose the occasion of a new millennium to preach on world peace. A year later, the Reverend R. Scott Colglazier, a leading Disciples of Christ minister, included the sermon in a collection he edited titled Yes to Peace, *offering me the perfect opportunity to express how relevant theological universalism is to the demands of a new century in a rapidly changing world.*

So here we are. Our computers still work. The world didn't end. Until the day after we die, tomorrow will always come, just as the day before it did. Day after day, the world plays in traffic and we hope we don't get hit. A new millennium has begun and almost none of us got hit. Is there a lesson here, a millennial lesson, something we didn't know before? Might thousands of fireworks celebrations (on the hour for twenty-four hours somewhere in the world) remind us of what we hope we yet might learn about life together on this planet?

Two thousand years ago, a prophet was born in Israel, with this angelic harbinger: "Peace on earth." Two millennia later are we any closer to realizing this dream, even those of us who follow the prophet, who try to live our lives according to his teachings? Looking forward from the close of the bloodiest century in history, what are the chances that peace on earth will one day turn from a dream to a reality? If the old idealism becomes the new realism, the chances, while still long, are not as crazy as you might think.

Since nothing happens in a vacuum, I shall begin by going back fifty years to the man whom I would name person of the last century, Franklin Delano Roosevelt. In his address to Congress on January 6, 1941, Roosevelt memorably and lastingly sketched out a global vision based on the attainment of four essential freedoms.

The first is freedom of speech and expression—everywhere in the world.

The second is freedom of every person to worship God in his own way—everywhere in the world.

The third is freedom from want, which, translated into world terms, means economic understandings which will secure to every nation a healthy peacetime life for its inhabitants—everywhere in the world.

The fourth is freedom from fear, which, translated into world terms, means a worldwide reduction of armaments to such a point and in such a thorough fashion that no nation will be in a position to commit an act of physical aggression against any neighbor—anywhere in the world.

Roosevelt went on to say, "This nation has placed its destiny in the hands and heads and hearts of its millions of free men and women, and its faith in freedom under the guidance of God. Freedom means the supremacy of human rights everywhere. Our support goes to those who struggle to gain those rights and keep them. Our strength is our unity of purpose."

Before Roosevelt delivered this deservedly celebrated address, he invited comments from his senior staff. Harry Hopkins, one of the president's principal advisers, questioned the phrase "everywhere in the world."

"That covers an awful lot of territory, Mr. President," he said. "I don't know how interested Americans are going to be in the people of Java."

Roosevelt's reply proved prescient. "I'm afraid they'll have to be some day, Harry. The world is getting so small that even the people in Java are getting to be our neighbors now."

In 1945, as countries were rising from the ashes of World War II, representatives from around the globe met in San Francisco to begin working on a charter for a new international peace organization, the United Nations. Among them was another renowned liberal, Franklin Roosevelt's wife, Eleanor. Tireless champion for the poor during her husband's thirteen years as president, she went on to serve as a delegate to the United Nations, chaired its Human Rights Commission, and coauthored the Universal Declaration of Human Rights. For her, the United Nations represented "the greatest hope for a peaceful world. . . . We must use all the knowledge we possess, all the avenues for seeking agreement and international understanding—not only for our own good, but for the good of all human beings."

Both a small- and a large-D democrat, Eleanor Roosevelt also possessed a liberal Christian temperament. An Episcopalian in the tradition of her uncle Theodore Roosevelt (though lacking his muscular bellicosity), in following Jesus she centered her practical faith on the second great commandment, to love thy neighbor as thyself. "Denominations mean little to me," she said in an interview shortly before she died. "If we pattern our lives on the life of Christ and sincerely try to follow his creed of compassion and love as expressed in the Sermon on the Mount we will find that sectarianism means less and less. . . . To me, the way your personal religion makes you live is the only thing that really matters." Her favorite passage in the King James Bible was 1 Corinthians 13:13: "And now abideth faith, hope, charity, these three; but the greatest of these is charity."

Hardheaded pundits argue that one cannot cobble together a program for society on the basis of charity, compassion, and neighborliness. They fail to notice one thing. The world is changing. Our founders' ideals, drawn from the scriptures and the laws of nature's God, are less fanciful today than ever before. Today, as Franklin Roosevelt predicted, we are challenged by a new paradigm, markedly more encompassing than that suggested by White House policy moguls. Its symbol is the shrinking globe. One world is no longer only a vision; it is a reality.

The Chinese have an ideograph for the word "crisis" that might serve as the emblem for our time. It is composed of two symbols, word-pictures for danger and opportunity. In the crisis we face today, everything we do has global consequence. If the danger is obvious, the opportunity for a new way of living together as kin is equally promising. One cannot overemphasize the importance of this paradigm shift.

Historically, certain basic tenets of liberalism, especially those with ethical connotations, have been dismissed as idealistic. This is true even of the liberalism of Jesus, who taught us to love our enemies and our neighbors as ourselves. Throughout history, the realist could have responded, and often has, with tough-minded and not completely inappropriate derision. For centuries, in political or societal terms, the practical translation of Jesus's saying "If he asks for your cloak, give him your coat also" might well be "If you let your enemy have an inch, he will take a mile, and soon your children will be in thralldom to him."

Such opinions were based on solid experience. Competitive virtues such as fortitude were initially not individual but community virtues. Valor in protecting one's family, tribe, or state from enemies across the river was essential for the survival of one's people and culture. Today, however, whether one is speaking of war or the environment, to protect our families we must struggle to protect our erstwhile enemies' families as well.

The old idealism has therefore become the new realism. The old idealist dreams about Star Wars deterrence, indulges in nostalgia for the 1950s, carps about the dangers of letting down our guard, and fights to lower taxes regardless of the long-term cost to society. The new realist is busy painting out the boundaries between peoples, investing in the next generation, caring for the environment, and beating swords into sickles.

The new realist knows that today our survival depends on our neighbors' survival. In a nuclear age, in which global war is murder-suicide or genocide, the only way to win is not to war with one another. Faced with a global environmental threat, none of us have discrete backyards any longer. Every person on this planet is in jeopardy whether it is we, the Chinese, or the Brazilians who are despoiling the environment. And with the advent of a global economy, we are not strengthened but rather threatened by our neighbors' economic insecurity. For the first time in history, a market crash halfway around the world is like a tsunami, a great tidal wave that will surely come crashing down on our shore.

In response to today's global realities, the old nationalism is beginning to yield to a new ethic, championed by Franklin and Eleanor Roosevelt and perhaps best expressed and understood by some contemporary feminists. It is a nurturing ethic based on the family model. Competition is replaced by cooperation, and hierarchical structures are supplanted by relational ones. The new ethic has as its cornerstone not the individual, sovereign and free, but rather the community.

In both geopolitical and national terms, to emphasize individual liberties at the expense of social relationships is increasingly dysfunctional. Our own freedom and liberty depend existentially and ontologically on justice being done for and shared with as many others as possible, regardless of politics or ethnic background. Not that we should sacrifice personal liberty; we should simply modulate it in such a way that our neighbors, too, are served. We must move from a foundation of atomic individualism to one of community and love.

Today the old I win/you lose, tribal or individualistic model is dysfunctional, if not obsolete. A new model, based on the family, suggests new metaphors for meaning: the earth as organism, the interdependent web, the kinship of all life. These metaphors are far more faithful to contemporary reality than the old, with God the Father, lord, and warrior undergirding the patriarchy and invoked by priest and ruler alike to justify the hierarchical structures and competitive systems that sustain it.

In her modern classic, *In a Different Voice*, feminist author and psychologist Carol Gilligan defines community according to an "ethic of care." The concept of identity expands to include the experience of interconnection. The moral domain is similarly enlarged by the inclusion of responsibility and care in relationships. And the underlying epistemology correspondingly shifts from the Greek ideal of knowledge as a correspondence between mind and form to the biblical conception of knowing as a process of human relationship.

Biblically resonant and family based, Gilligan's model for community offers a redemptive new metaphor for contemporary liberals. Those who speak in the woman's "different voice" form the potential vanguard of a new world, not a brave new world but a more compassionate one. Challenging the rough-and-tumble, lift-yourself-up-by-your-own-bootstraps ethic, they shift our attention from the atomic individual to the community of individuals, people who share common needs that can be fulfilled only through mutual nurture and support. To suggest that such a world could ever be born may seem utopian. We have a terrible time living with our neighbors' differences, whether of color, nationality, or faith. But that takes nothing away from the truth, even the practicality of such ideals. If we possess an instinct for survival, such tonics as relationship, nurture, and mutual respect contain saving power.

Think of it in terms of enlightened self-interest. Once neighborhoods were insulated and prejudices functional for societal bonding. Today we are thrown, in all our glorious and troublesome diversity, into one another's backyards. We can attempt to convert or subdue our neighbors by imposing a dominant set of values, but this form of cultural or religious imperialism invites its own whiplash. As the world shrinks and populations mix, traditional worldviews, whether sponsored by the European men who brought us Western culture or the mullahs who wield the sword of Allah, will only continue to dominate at everyone's peril, including their own. In a pluralistic world, the fundamentalist or ideologue will either go the way of the dinosaur or bring himself down as he brings down his neighbor. Although our penchant for division, tension, and destruction is manifested daily, if we possess an instinct for survival, over time we shall adapt to these new realities.

Universalist values are essential today for another reason. The world may be shrinking, but we will never be clones of one another. We can build community only by respecting differences, sometimes major differences. This means educating ourselves in the ways, traditions, and cultures of the other, who lives no longer across the world but right next door. It also means changing the way we live with and listen to one another, not as competing families but as members of a single, fascinating (if inevitably somewhat dysfunctional) family containing a myriad of hues, customs, and beliefs.

This is not abdication. It is the promised realization of principles on which this liberal democracy was founded, principles inspired by the spirit of the scriptures and read in the text of creation. All are created equal, not alike, but equal. All have certain inalienable rights. Among the freedoms we most avidly protect are the freedoms of religion and speech. The only way to ensure our liberty is to protect the liberty of our neighbor as well. In a pluralistic world that means respecting, even honoring, differences. This mandate is reinforced daily, as we become more cognizant of our interdependencies. Each part, every individual, faith, color, and nationality is distinct, but one mother holds us all to her bosom, giving us life, providing us a home—the Commonwealth of God.

As Shug says of God in Alice Walker's *The Color Purple*, "My first step away from the old white man was trees. Then air. Then birds. Then other people. But one day when I was sitting quiet and feeling like a motherless child, which I was, it come to me: that feeling of being part of everything, not separate at all."

Peace on earth. In America we have a name for it: *E pluribus unum.* Out of many, one. It's a universalist epiphany.

CHAPTER 13

Choose Life

The drama playing out during Easter week 2005 involved a national debate over whether a woman, Terri Schiavo, should be taken off life support after fifteen years and allowed to die. Not only were her family members and doctors involved, but a religious campaign had stirred Congress to vote on the matter. I rarely preach to awaken my congregation to the importance of social issues they evince no interest in—such preaching is presumptuous and ineffective—but when something tragic happens in my city, country, or world, arresting universal sympathy and pain, or the entire nation is involved in an ethical debate, I toss my planned sermon away and weigh in. It just so happened that Easter provided the perfect occasion to reflect on love and death through the lens of this public life-and-death drama.

The great Christian ethicist Reinhold Niebuhr instructed his ministerial students at Union Theological Seminary to preach with the Bible in one hand and the newspaper in the other. Half a century later, with the Bible making daily headlines as members of Congress routinely cite God and the scriptures when shaping public policy, his concern that the newspaper might be neglected by preachers seems almost quaint. These days anyone seeking spiritual guidance can go straight to the newspaper, beginning on page one, on through the

Nation section, and continuing through the op-ed pages. Given the taut twist fundamentalist religion is giving to public policy discussions, I'm quite sure that Professor Niebuhr would have lavished more than a little of his delicious irony on today's religious politics.

On the other hand, that the entire nation should focus on the life-and-death drama of a single individual during Easter week does direct our thoughts where they probably ought to be. I have nothing but compassion for the parties most intimately involved in the Terri Schiavo case. My heart goes out to Terri herself, whose life as we know life (mindful, sentient, and purposeful) appears effectively to have ended fifteen years ago; to her parents, who, understandably, continue to hope against hope that she might yet miraculously recover; to her husband, whose years of unanswered prayers have finally reconciled him to the futility of prolonging Terri's subsistence; to her doctors, who deliberated long and hard before determining that to keep Terri's body alive any longer would not serve life, but only prolong her living death; and to the judges, before whom the settlement of her case properly lies. One may question their decision to let Mrs. Schiavo die, while remaining grateful that we live in a nation of secular laws and not in a theocracy.

I wish I could add that my compassion (always an elevating sentiment) extends to the politicians who have opportunistically seized upon this family tragedy to trumpet their piety. Jesus warned against public displays of piety. He knew that self-righteous display is the opposite of righteousness before God. Among other things, such displays promote hypocrisy.

Today, with respect to our born-again Congress, this hypocrisy is most evident in the ongoing debate over next year's budget. Medicaid largely underwrites Terri Schiavo's care and that of others like her, even as national funding for health care is being frozen and may soon be slashed. One can make a moral case against all forms of euthanasia, but to do so responsibly requires a commitment to underwrite the massive costs such a position must entail.

As for all the pious political expostulation against starving this poor woman to death, votes cast to cut back on food stamps here at home or slicing foreign aid to abate famine abroad rip out untold numbers of feeding tubes. Children daily die in Africa by the hundreds, by the thousands, without fanfare, children not in a vegetative state, who might otherwise have lived a full and active life. While ignoring or rejecting so many other humanitarian pleas, when our legislators take time off from cutting the human services budget to promote a feeding law designed to address the plight of a single human being, they turn the right-wing "culture of life" mantra into a parody.

The Terri Schiavo controversy has led to at least one positive outcome. Over the past week, several of you (perhaps many of you) have amended your living wills explicitly to include feeding tubes in the category of artificial life supports you ask not be employed to prolong your life beyond its natural term. My wife, Carolyn, and I have done the same. We would readily choose death over fifteen years of vegetative or semivegetative life supported by tubes. Death is not a curse to be outwitted no matter the cost. Death is the natural pivot on which life turns, without which life as we know it could not be. A pro-life-support position is not always a pro-life position. When we can no longer hold on with hope or purpose, to let go is to die with dignity and grace.

It goes without saying that the pro-life rubric provides the religious right with a powerful rhetorical symbol. The word "life" encompasses a far more resonant standard for moral action than does the word "choice." And yet, in the book of Deuteronomy, when Moses tells God's people, "Choose Life," life and choice are yoked together in a single redemptive dynamic. Without choice, life, especially moral life, is diminished to almost nothing. Without choice there can be no moral agency. Moral capacity is based entirely on the ability to choose, even to choose life. By definition, a life-affirming ethic requires hard choices among competing moral ideals. For instance, the social cost of banning all forms of euthanasia (considered a mortal sin by the religious right) will be offset elsewhere, at the expense of prenatal care or of preventative medicine. Some proportion of healthy people will become mortally ill in exchange for keeping a smaller number of critically ill people barely alive. To choose life, embracing the fullness of God's call, we must be morally mature enough to admit the necessity of triage. Otherwise, on the altar of our piety we may lavish care on those who can't significantly be helped, while others, whose lives might be saved at far less cost, languish in the nation's expanding waiting room.

With respect to abortion, did you know that three hundred thousand fewer abortions were performed during President Clinton's eight years in office than have already occurred during President Bush's first five? In part, this is surely due to the cutback in funding and the restriction of birth control and family planning services in health education and sex education programs.

In light of these numbers, one could argue that a pro-choice agenda serves the anti-abortion cause more effectively than does a so-called pro-life agenda, which limits contraceptive options and restricts sex education to the moralistic platitude of "Just say no." Even apart from such evidence, a pro-birth stance outlawing all forms of abortion and an anti-death stance outlawing all forms of euthanasia (though rarely extended to capital punishment and war) does not, in my opinion, add up to a pro-life policy, especially when questions addressing the quality of life (after birth and before death) appear to evoke respectively little moral intensity or compassionate solicitude from many self-described pro-life crusaders. Beyond this, if we are truly to choose life, we must weigh the competing demands for our moral attention in the scales of equity and justice. An encompassing pro-life position would weigh into the balance poverty and malnutrition, equal health care and education, and all the many facets of human rights and dignity, with as much care as today's pro-life crusaders devote to abortion, euthanasia, and same-sex marriage.

To choose life is not, regardless of the cost, to mandate birth or to prevent death. To choose life is to nurture and enhance the quality of life for the entire human family. This entails moral choice and requires moral compromise. No responsible civil ethic can be fashioned that does not allow prioritizing the competing claims on our moral attention. To choose life (reverently and thoughtfully, unbiased by sentimentality), we must resist the siren's song of moral absolutists, for whom both choice and compromise are anathema.

I recognize that I've been talking about ethics on what many would define as a metaphysical occasion. Before mounting my spiritual charger, as all these Easter trumpets seem to call for, and galloping off toward the ether, let me say a word about our approach to religion here in this church.

We Unitarian Universalists are sometimes accused of having a thick ethic and a thin metaphysic. Even on Easter, I will rush to say, "Guilty as charged." We test our faith by deeds, not creeds. As Henry David Thoreau put it when asked about the afterlife, we prefer to take things one life at a time. Our book of revelation is the book of nature. We read the story of our lives and the story of life itself in its rich and luxuriant pages. As Jesus himself did, we follow the spirit, not the letter, of the scriptures. Love to God, the God of many names, and love to neighbor, sum up all the law and the prophets. Whatever we may think about life after death, we devote our full spiritual attentions to life before death, seeking to live in such a way that our lives will prove worth dying for. When pondering the life and death of Terri Schiavo or Jesus of Nazareth or our own life and death, we look not to the supernatural for meaning or rescue. Instead, we peer through life's veil for a glimpse of the super in the natural, that our lives may be touched by awe and blessed by grace.

By definition, questions of ultimate meaning are religious questions. One may answer them, of course, with nonreligious answers. Just make sure that these answers are not too glib. If fundamentalists of the right enshrine an idol on their altar, an impossibly petty, tyrannical, and tiny God, fundamentalists of the left strike that idol from the altar and believe that they have done something creative or important. Both remain in thralldom to the same tiny God.

Perhaps it's time to gaze into the heavens, to recognize that we are all more alike than we differ, certainly more alike in our ignorance than we differ in our knowledge. Time to remember how fragile life is and how precious love must therefore be. Time to seize every opportunity we are given to offer thanks, to celebrate, to serve, hope, and love. Perhaps it's time to wander back once again to Calvary for our annual Easter visit. Nothing is there now. No crosses. No crowd. We stand alone, looking beyond a naked hill to an endless desert. You and I together, each of us alone, looking out on eternity, measuring time. Alone together with Terri and with Jesus and with one another. We look into forever and we weep.

And then we look back. How amazing it was! Wasn't it amazing? The people who loved us. The people who tried. Our parents, they weren't perfect, no, but neither are we. Our children, if we are blessed to have children. Our friends, the sun and moon, touch and sight, taste, hearing, smell, every miracle we take for granted every day of our lives until the day we die. How amazing it was, life before death. Look ahead and mourn. Then look back and sing. Remember how profoundly we are blessed. Yes, and then we too are resurrected. Removed from our death supports.

Whatever our theology, Jesus lived to remind us that we, too, can be saved. Not from others, but from ourselves. Saved from self-absorption, self-pity, self-hatred. Saved from self-righteousness. Saved from unwarranted displays of conspicuous piety. Saved by love.

Let me leave you with a question. What if this is your last Easter? Or the last Easter you are blessed to share with someone you love? Will anything you do or feel today remain? In your heart you know the answer. Only love remains, only the love we give away, the rest is dross.

For you and for me, for Jesus and for Peter, for Terri and her parents and her husband, when death is the occasion, love is the only saving medium, and forgiveness, love's most perfect catalyst. That is the message of Easter, its hope and its promise. Death doesn't conquer love; love conquers death. Those who love us live on in the love we receive. By their love we shall always know them. And our own bequest of love, however imperfect, this too will outlast us. It will outlast us and it will perfect us. For not only does the love we give live on in our name. It redeems our own and saves our loved ones' lives.

You won't find that in the newspapers. But you will in the Bible. "Choose Life." "Love your neighbor as yourself."

Can you imagine anything more amazing? Life before death. And then love after death. Each is miracle enough for me. Each sufficient cause for everlasting praise.

CHAPTER 14

Evil and Sin

One issue confronted by all theologians is the question of good and evil. It lies at the very heart of every form of dualism and gnosticism. Christianity posits a fallen angel, Lucifer or the devil, to explain evil's power over God's creation. Known for its generous spirit, liberal theology has traditionally been weak on the subject of evil. Motivated by news reports in 2006 of the torture of Iraqi detainees by American soldiers at Abu Ghraib prison, I wrote this sermon (excerpted here) to address that weakness.

Some religious liberals cringe at the word "evil." I don't. Adolf Hitler, Joseph Stalin, Saddam Hussein, and Osama bin Laden are not basically good people who sometimes did or do bad things: they and the structures they erected to enforce their will and expand their power were and are agents and agencies of evil. This helps account for the predicament in which we, as a nation, now find ourselves. Our leaders are so outraged by the evil of our self-appointed and chosen adversaries, so blinded by the light in which their own and our nation's high moral idealism bathes them, that they cannot see—cannot even imagine—that we ourselves might cast a similar shadow.

The squalid revelations of prisoner abuse by U.S. troops at the Abu Ghraib prison in Iraq and the grotesque beheading of American contract worker Nicholas Berg as an act of direct retaliation have been a wakeup call, a reminder that being American, despite this nation's lofty ideals, doesn't immunize us from sponsoring evil.

National or collective sin almost always cloaks self-interest in the garb of higher virtue. Not only as individuals but also as a nation, we justify questionable means by noble ends. We exculpate ourselves by pointing out that others do worse. We rationalize away our crimes as aberrant. In short, by shifting moral responsibility away from ourselves, we pronounce ourselves innocent. Ever since Adam blamed Eve and Eve blamed the serpent, we humans have avoided taking responsibility for our actions (and therefore accountability for their consequences) by proclaiming that the buck stops elsewhere. That, in a nutshell, is original sin.

Liberal theology doesn't take sin and evil seriously enough. American fundamentalism takes evil seriously, and would certainly seem to have a doctrine of sin. But by trivializing sin into a moralistic catalogue of personal foibles, fundamentalists often appear to reserve the badge of real evil for others. With sin, however, there are no others. The world is not divided into sheep and goats. Each of us is both sheep and goat, making original sin a corrective to any theology based on an "us versus them" model, and conducive as well to the development of a clear-eyed, unsentimental universalism. Martin Luther put it this way: "The ultimate human sin is our unwillingness to concede that we are sinners."

Al-Qaeda terrorist Abu Musab al-Zarqawi and his henchmen beheaded Nick Berg, recording it on videotape in retaliation for the brutal, humiliating treatment of Iraqi prisoners in Abu Ghraib prison, itself captured on video. Events in Iraq tragically prove the first law of history: choose your enemies carefully, for you will become like them.

What happened in Abu Ghraib does "not represent America," our president said. And he is right. It represents human nature. It's not only that good people sometimes do bad things or that in every barrel there are a few bad apples, but that the veneer of civilized behavior is thin, fragile, and of relatively recent application. There has never been a war in which we humans have not dehumanized our enemies, leading the victors to treat the vanquished like animals. And barring strict internal controls and external oversight, prisons are, almost by definition, inhumane. Under stress, especially when we mull in crowds or small packs, human behavior easily becomes wanton and brutal—bestial, we proclaim, though animals are almost never what we refer to as inhumane to one another.

If you don't like the word "sin," substitute another—"humankind's innate inhumanity," perhaps—but don't underestimate the concept, or think that we are all born good and then somehow get destroyed or twisted by society. Given our natural egotism and instinct for survival, which through opportunistic self-rationalization easily morph into the drive to dominate, sin is bred in the human bone.

The founders of our nation certainly understood this. They knew that, unchecked by moral and state stricture, people act in their own self-interest, mindless of the common good. The founders weren't cynics. They knew that we humans, as the Bible says, are at once scarcely higher than the beasts and just a little lower than the angels. Blessed with high ideals yet tempered by realism, they crafted our government with an eye both to the intrinsic potential dignity and the inevitable corruption of human nature. Their ideals set this nation under a remarkably, perhaps impossibly, high set of standards: liberty and justice for all. At the same time, they attended to the lesser angels of our nature, deftly establishing a balance between competing factions and interests to ensure that no group, neither a majority nor a minority, could impose its will unchecked by competing interests. By cutting corners, today's leaders chip away at the nation's cornerstones.

We have so much more in common than could ever possibly divide us: alike mysteriously born and fated to die, the same sun setting on each of our horizons. We all want and need love, security, freedom, and acceptance. We need others' forgiveness and understanding. All of us do. We ache in the same way. We bleed in the same way. At times, we all feel awkward and unworthy and inadequate. And we all fail at times to hearken to the better angels of our nature.

This is the centerpiece of theological universalism. To whatever extent we place our primary identification with sect or nation, with race or gender, with school or party, we betray our common humanity. Party to faction, we fall prey to the beguiling logic of division, the logic of retribution and judgment, the logic of hate. In short, we live—all of us live—riddled with sin and in need of salvation. These two tenets of universalist theology complement each other. It's worth remembering, in a world defined by the rhetoric of "us versus them," that we, too, are sinners and that they, too, can be saved.

CHAPTER 15

Religion and the Body Politic

I close this sample of universalist sermons from my liberal pulpit with my Election Day sermon from 2008. As the most historic and important presidential campaign in recent history was hurtling toward a close, I returned to the early Puritans, who established the election sermon as a genre in the early seventeenth century.

There's a noble tradition in the ministry, going back to the seventeenth century. One or two Sundays before an election, almost every preacher in the land devoted his sermon to the body politic.

It's a great literary genre. Often, the brimstone was so fiery hot that an Election Day sermon was the one sermon a minister might be remembered by. There was a reason for that. No words were minced. He entered the pulpit and for the next two hours—count your blessings, folks—proclaimed a jeremiad (the word is from Jeremiah, the great Hebrew prophet).

Here's how it went. The world has gone, or is about to go, to hell. The reason is simple. God is punishing you for your sins. Whatever is wrong in this world is wrong because you are wrongheaded, wronghearted, inattentive to God's commandments, and God is watching and God is angry, and if you keep on messing up you will burn forever.

At least they burned for two long hours. Nonetheless, by the end of the pastor's jeremiad, almost everyone who listened did in fact feel at least partially responsible for everything that was going wrong in the world. No more "throw the bums out"; the bums were us.

In passing judgment and in their demands for moral perfection, the early Puritan preachers too often forgot the importance of forgiveness: of loving-kindness; of self-acceptance; of honest doubts. But they did remind us that, despite our failings, we are accountable. They didn't let us pass the buck while complaining that somebody else was diminishing its value.

I won't give you two hours' worth of sermon, and I'm not going to tell you who to vote for. I'm not even going to tell you that everything wrong with this country is your fault and the result of God's responsive wrath.

I will say, however, with the nation mired in two seemingly endless wars and the economy in meltdown, that this is the most important presidential election since 1932.

Add the almost unimaginable, world-inspiring presence of an African American on the verge of being elected president of the United States—or the first female candidate being elected vice president— and the election takes on a historic quality unparalleled in modern memory.

With the world on a precipice and our economy in ruins, we will be casting the most critical vote of our lifetimes. In casting this vote, one question should rest foremost in our minds. Which of the two candidates is most likely to spend his first one hundred days emulating Franklin Delano Roosevelt?

There wasn't a hint of FDR's first one hundred days in his generic, quite negative campaign for president, during which he stressed the importance of balancing the federal budget. But then, almost overnight, with the prompt action of a willing Congress, he corrected the nation's course and charted a new future for America.

Only George Washington and Abraham Lincoln faced so huge a challenge. The former met it by making the founders' dreams come true, the latter, over four long years, by ending slavery.

Our next president will face a challenge less monumental than these, perhaps, but certainly greater than any we have faced in recent decades. He must rise to the occasion and we must rise with him. If he fails to rise, it is our responsibility to present not a partisan but a patriotic demand that he and the Congress put aside their base-pleasing talking points and act on behalf of all the American people: first, by making the hard decisions that will right our economy; and second, by conducting our foreign policy in a way that will make our nation and our allies once again proud of America at its best.

In the spirit, if not the letter, of our Puritan forebears let me expand my compass to include a religious charge. Both the candidates for office are flawed men. I accept that. I want a flawed person in the White House, but one who knows that he or she is flawed. The reason is simple. The president will be less dangerous. Certitude, moral and otherwise, is blind. For eight long years we have witnessed the ravages of moral certitude and blind, inflexible leadership. We can't afford, and the world can't afford, more of the same.

That said, the president of the United States alone is not going to save us. The votes we cast for president are far less important than the votes we cast with and in our lives. Then God, greater than all and yet present in each, will save us. God will save us by looking through our eyes, and touching our hearts, and applying our hands to the saving work of neighborly love. Conversely, wherever you see neighborly hate, God is absent. God's love unites us, it doesn't divide us, either within or among ourselves.

If the United States of America is about anything it is about unity amid diversity. Not one for many, but out of many, one. It is far less important that the trains run on time, even that all the passengers have a government-stamped ticket, than that the passengers are willing to take responsibility for one another's welfare.

On this historic election eve, the choice we must make, not just with our vote, but with our lives, is a choice between hope and fear. Hate is not love's opposite, fear is. When we are frightened—by others, by life itself—we cannot love. We can hide. We can fight. But we cannot love. Conversely, love casts out fear.

We are good at fear. That's why politicians play on our fears. Fear divides, weakens, and then conquers us. It feeds on our weakness and envy and jealousy. It leads us to follow those who tell us we are victims. It closes hearts and poisons minds.

One of the ways fear drives the world today may, on its face, seem positive. Fear loves order and hates disorder. Fear will sacrifice equity and freedom for order in a minute. I'm not suggesting that disorder is good and order bad. Both are neutral in value. All depends on the ingredients that create them. But, in the spirit of the founders, controlled disorder is far more American than imposed order. Imposed order almost always rises phoenix-like from the ashes of scapegoats. Jews, gays, feminists, blacks, immigrants: take your pick.

Let me close this brief and gentle jeremiad by recalling the basic ingredients of the religious life. Saint Paul named the three great virtues: faith, hope, and love. If fear is love's opposite, the opposite of faith is belief, and the opposite of hope is certitude.

Faith is confidence, a basic trust in being. Belief is a set of propositions that true believers claim make it possible for us to possess faith. In fact, belief diminishes faith's compass. It may even kill faith. We believe something, or in someone, and it disappoints us or they disappoint us and we lose our faith.

Belief has a second shadow side. How easily it becomes demonic, or even silly. Take the pastor who said that, since Buddhists, Hindus, and Muslims around the world were praying for an Obama victory, if McCain didn't win, our God would look smaller than theirs.

Belief casts a psychological shadow as well. Surely each of us has believed at some point in someone, but then followed three assassinations, Vietnam, Watergate. Times changed or we changed. Camelot came and went and we lost our faith. We became cynical. Or we lurched from one belief system to another. It's an old, familiar story. Think of how many ex-communists joined the Catholic Church. The God who failed fails again and again and again. Faith, which says yes to mystery, wonder, possibility, and change, should never be sacrificed to belief.

For instance, I have faith in myself, but I certainly don't believe in myself. Only faith can get us through a dark night of the soul. It's the difference between a view and a fortress, the difference between horizons and walls.

As for hope, the opposite of hope is certitude. Hope says that things can perhaps be different, be better, the world and ourselves redeemed, if only we will align ourselves with life by doing what we can and being who we yet might be. Hopelessness is one form of certitude. Assurance is another. Both squeeze out the gentle ambiguities of hope.

I don't want my president to crush my hope by setting up an impossible dream, any more than I want to succumb to the cynics who have lost their ability to dream. Instead I want my president to inspire hope. I want him to justify my faith in him. And I certainly want him to encourage not my fears but my love.

Mine is a religious request. I know that. But, after all, this is a religious nation, an experiment in religious freedom, founded in the spirit, not the letter, of the scriptures. As we near Election Day, I am no more ashamed of making a religious request than my forebears were when they fulminated for hours, expressing as sincere a desire that everything, somehow, might turn out right.

I ask a lot, because our founders and early leaders asked no less of us. The United States of America is the most daring experiment in democratic governance that has ever been fashioned. Our responsibilities are equal to its promise. I have great faith in our system of government. I love this country and its people. I hope that our future will fulfill the founders' dreams.

Yes, I have my doubts. And I have my fears. All of us do. Yet my faith and hope are strong. We who already have so much will somehow muster the capacity to rise to historic occasions such as this one. If we and our leaders can somehow rise beyond politics as usual to meet this momentous challenge, November 4 will mark not the end of this election. It will mark its beginning. And the world will change.

BOOK IV

Universalism for the
Twenty-first Century

CHAPTER 16

The Search for Meaning

One summer in the late 1980s, I was asked to spend a week facilitating a session at the Aspen Institute, in Aspen, Colorado. Author Phillip Berman was in Aspen, also, doing interviews for a compendious, fascinating book, which he titled The Search for Meaning: Americans Talk About What They Believe and Why. *In my case, Berman condensed a wide-ranging two-hour conversation into a brief monologue, one which fairly encapsulates a number of my beliefs, both then and today, in a breezy way. Rediscovering this interview recently, I was reminded how little my liberal faith, once grounded in universalism, has changed over the years. One, not insignificant, exception to this rule is my shift from "Kingdom" to "Commonwealth" language when speaking of God's realm. What surprised me most was to discover implicit here the mantra by which I've lived the last decade of my life: "Want what you have; do what you can; be who you are." There is one overarching difference, however. What I believed then mostly in my mind, today I embrace with all my heart.*

I was raised a Presbyterian, sort of an ice-cream-social Presbyterian, high holidays and nice clothes, but not at all serious. As I remember it, one of the keys to success for a Presbyterian Sunday schooler in those days was being able to color Jesus in a meaningful way. I wasn't very good at art, so I had a hard time keeping the sky out of his face. If my religion had ended there, by certain theological standards, anyway, I would have failed.

The key experience or transforming early religious moment for me was when my father, Frank Church, was elected to the U.S. Senate. He was given a Bible, *Jefferson's Bible*. During his time in the White House, Thomas Jefferson took the Gospels and excerpted those passages that he found most worthy, compelling, and enduring, and cut out the rest. He cut out the virgin birth and resurrection. *Jefferson's Bible* ends with the rolling of the stone against the tomb. It was the first Bible I'd ever really read, all words, no pictures. I found myself gripped by the human Jesus.

As represented in *Jefferson's Bible*, Jesus had no miraculous birth or miraculous death. He lived, by force of example and the power of his teaching, a miraculous life. As I grew older, I began to realize that we couldn't emulate Jesus in his supposed birth, because our births were natural. And we couldn't emulate him in our deaths, because our deaths will be natural. But we could, if we were to study his teachings, be transformed by them and, to a small degree at least, emulate his life. Our challenge was, in the same way that he did, to live our lives in such a way that they would be worth dying for.

That stuck with me, and through my time at Harvard I gradually gravitated toward Unitarian Universalism, only then discovering that Jefferson himself had been a unitarian. So there was a kind of coherence in my developing religious orientation, grounded back in that early experience of reading *Jefferson's Bible* and having religion for the first time really make sense to me. That finally prompted me to go into the Unitarian Universalist ministry. I don't think, however, that I truly became a grounded and thoughtful religious person until I left academia and began working in a church. And I'm not sure I became a minister until I presided over my first funeral.

My belief that religion is our human response to the dual reality of being alive and knowing we must die initially emerged from my experience with people who were dying, with families who were struggling. Each of us is a religious being. In death's shadow, we ponder who we are, why we live, what the purpose of our life is, where we come from, and where we are going. In this many-chambered crucible of bewilderment and wonder, our religion is forged.

I do fear dying, although I don't fear death. The great blessing of the ministry is that one is invited to participate all the time in the lives of people who are facing death and dying, and that does a couple of things. First of all it helps to put one's own petty problems, envies, jealousies, bitterness, anger, and strivings into perspective. These things are so unimportant compared to that ultimate passage. It blows all the dust off of one's psychological plate. And then one is invited fully to participate in the sacrament of death with others. I have seen enough people die to know that there is a potential in that passage for peace, for beauty, and for completion.

I live according to a few simple principles. One I call "nostalgia for the present" (embracing each day as it passes rather than ruing it after it's gone). Another way you might put this is "looking forward to the present" (enjoying what you have as if in a state of anticipation rather than aching longingly for that which very likely will not be). By focusing one's energy, to the extent that it is possible, on the present, one is liberated from fears of the future and also liberated from regrets about the past. I have seen people in the last weeks of their lives live every minute more fully than they ever have before, because they recognize what most of us don't in our daily living: that each moment is precious.

The opposite of wishful thinking (wishing for something you lack) is thoughtful wishing (thinking to wish for what you've got right now). What we have right now is this day with the wind blowing and the mottled light on the mountains in this beautiful place, carrying on a conversation with another human being who is also going to die. It's very precious. It's a miracle that we're even able to converse. We tend, I think, to take our lives for granted rather than receiving them daily as a gift. I would hope that each day I live I might, through some encounter, be born again to an awareness and appreciation for the gift of life, the mystery of being, the wonder and the miracle. Not the miracle out there, but the miracle in here.

To this extent, I follow in the spirit of Jesus. Our lives find their meaning to the extent that we empty ourselves and are filled, lose ourselves and are found, give ourselves away to others and find ourselves in our encounter with them, without which there is nothing but isolation and self-absorption and ultimately estrangement and emptiness.

I find myself guided in my own thinking more and more by paradox. My definition of the devil, for instance, is evil disguised as good. My definition of angels, messengers of the divine, is goodness disguised in ordinary encounters or wrapped in brown paper. I try to be most suspicious of my finest actions, to be most wary of my most compelling thoughts, and always to try to find something redemptive in the thoughts or actions of others.

Two keys to religious living are humility and openness. Some people will take a look at how little they can finally know and either give up or make a leap of faith that answers all those unanswerable questions so they don't have to think anymore. Other people will sense the dangers of openness and batten themselves down. But if you work the two principles together, remaining humble about how little we possibly can know while remaining open to how the sky is the limit in terms of our growth, there is a dynamic to life that is wondrous.

I say to my congregants, "If you believe in God, the best thing you can do for yourself is to suspend your belief for a while, because undoubtedly your God is too small and you must grow beyond that God. On the other hand, if you don't believe in God, your very disbelief is a stumbling block. Kick it away and place your faith in something, in something more ennobling than disbelief. Take a flier. Expand your purview. Take a leap of faith."

Get to this point and there is no end to the openings for growth. The only way we grow is by changing. This is one of the reasons why we learn more from people who are radically different from us than we do from people who are like us. Our tendency instead is to group according to prejudice in tribes and then to close the other out. People with AIDS, for instance. We're not only frightened of disease; we're frightened of difference. We're frightened of having our pet prejudices challenged. The moment you become too sure of your beliefs, you really ought to spill them out, tip them over, mess them around, throw some new things in so as not to become a victim of your own prejudices.

Belief is self-ratifying and disbelief is self-ratifying. We tend to see what we look for, but as Jesus points out, the Kingdom of God is not where you're going to be looking for it. The Kingdom of God is in a mustard seed, the least portentous of all seeds. The Kingdom of God is not revealed by the good son but by the prodigal son. It's revealed by prostitutes and tax collectors. Depending on your prejudices, the parable of the good Samaritan is the parable of the good homosexual with AIDS or the parable of the good redneck with a gun in the back of his truck. The Kingdom of God is revealed where you least expect to find it.

So it's pretty simple for me: Love when you can. Do the work that is yours to do. Be the person that is yours to be at any given time. Think to wish for what is yours at this very moment. To love. To serve. To touch. To know. Think to wish for all that is yours to have. Think to wish for all that is yours to do. And think to wish that you might be who it is that you might most fully be. Avoid wishful thinking. Avoid the traps and pitfalls of nostalgia for the past. Savor every moment as it passes. And enlist yourself in saving that which can be saved this very moment, in order that it, too, may endure for others to enjoy.

CHAPTER 17

The Church of the Future in Light of the Past

By definition, modern universalism's religious centerpiece is nonsectarian. It rests in the belief that God is love and salvation is therefore shared, not reserved for one religious body or another. To expand our acquaintance with universalist theology, however, we can profitably tap the history of the Unitarian and Universalist denominations. In the United States, these two bodies have been debating the essence of universalism for some two centuries: the Universalists gathering in 1789; the Unitarians in 1825. I cut my theological teeth in a dialogue with my coreligionists, members of the (now linked) Unitarian Universalist Association. From the outset of my ministry, while inspired by the contributions of Unitarian prophets like Ralph Waldo Emerson, I have been equally drawn to more institutionally committed ministers like Henry Whitney Bellows, who challenged the Emersonian ideal of sovereign individualism. I open this section with three pieces initially addressed to my fellow Unitarian Universalists, the first delivered in 1979, the latter two almost a quarter century later.

To examine our institutional roots, I invite you to time-travel with me. The place is New York City. The year is 1865. The Civil War is over. Destruction has given way to reconstruction; fratricide, to a call for reconciliation. America is rising from its own ashes: the ashes of its children whose future was cut short by war; and the still smoldering memory of its slain president. This same year witnessed the emergence of a new corporate vision in both the Unitarian and the Universalist churches.

Among the Unitarians, my predecessor in the All Souls pulpit Henry Whitney Bellows was more responsible than any other individual in binding together a diverse religious constituency into a real denomination. In historian Conrad Wright's words, this great liberal churchman was "the one indispensable person in an enterprise that saved Unitarianism in America from atrophy and ultimate extinction." On completing his tenure as founder and head of the U.S. Sanitary Commission—forerunner of the Red Cross, Bellows's institution nursed the wounded on both sides during the Civil War—he placed as his new top priority the nurture of Unitarian institutions. Soon thereafter he would found the Unitarian Ministers' Association. In 1865 Bellows convened in New York the first meeting of the National Conference of Unitarian Churches.

Also in New York in 1865, Elbridge Gerry Brooks, minister of the Sixth Universalist Society, galvanized the heretofore-weak General Convention of Universalists into an effective denominational agency. As did Bellows, Brooks sought to enlarge the compass and ensure the ongoing vitality of his denomination. According to his Universalist contemporary Moses Ballou, "Brooks, more than almost any other person, organized the denomination in its present form, and to that institution, to that power in this country, he gave all that he had." The first meeting of the new Board of Trustees of the Universalist General Convention took place at Brooks's residence in September 1865. Two years later the board moved to enhance the denominational structure still further by appointing a general secretary, choosing for this post's first occupant Elbridge Gerry Brooks.

Many Unitarians and Universalists bristled at Bellows's and Brooks's efforts. They resisted any mechanism that might impinge on the principle of individual freedom. This resistance extended to both men's attempt to formulate a common (broad but more coherent) institutional foundation for their faith. As Universalist minister

I.D. Williamson said in opposing Brooks, "Our people, schooled in our great Protestant principle, will plant themselves on the responsibility to God alone, and let the doings of association and conventions pass unheeded."

Elbridge Brooks and Henry Bellows both saw their task as building the church of the future. In 1865 they played pivotal roles sparking strikingly parallel developments in their respective denominations. Their visions of how the church of the future might look, however, were by no means the same. In his sermon "The Suspense of Faith," Bellows called for a new Catholicism, one as inclusive as the name (meaning "universal") suggests. Brooks strongly disagreed. In his book *Our New Departure*, he argued that "the Church of the Future is to be a vitalized Protestant Church, and not a rejuvenated Roman Catholic Church with the Pope left out." Yet both men were reacting to a destructive exaggeration of individual freedom within their respective communions, leading to a neglect of corporate responsibility and a failure to attend to the cultivation of a larger community of faith. As church historian George Huntston Williams writes in his bicentennial essay on the history of *American Universalism* (in words that could equally be applied to Bellows):

> Brooks had to acknowledge that in large measure Universalism had undergone "some of the worst influences" of fissiparous evangelical congregationalism and individualism, but he was somehow confident that Universalism as now emerging could help the world understand "the Church as the perpetual symbol of religious ideas and as the means of communicating spiritual life."

Brooks could be eloquent on this subject. "The old theologies are dying," he preached. "Souls are adrift; minds are questioning and doubting. Hearts are hungering. Life is largely without centre or mastery, except from beneath. What [people] need is spiritual arrest, quickening, anchorage. Ours it is, if we actually have any business in the world, to answer these great uses."

If I took the time to quote Brooks and Bellows more generously, it would become obvious that theirs is a narrower faith than most Unitarian Universalists profess today. Contemporary Unitarian Universalists resonate more naturally with those who fought these two institutionalists tooth and nail. To repudiate our visionaries and prophets, mavericks of a century ago, would to many in our association be unthinkable. And, indeed, more spiritual by nature than Henry Whitney Bellows, transcendentalists like Ralph Waldo Emerson significantly expanded the theological compass of liberal religion.

What we can learn from Bellows and Brooks is that the gospel of freedom alone is not enough. Freedom of religion too easily translates into the emptiness of freedom from religion. Without strong and vigorous structures, vital worshipping communities, and a faith that sustains more than a self-satisfied few through times of crisis and hardship, our much vaunted freedom and openness remain spiritless abstractions. We must not forget that what we offer is an alternative religion (one modified and shaped by the principles of freedom and open process), not an alternative to religion.

Our challenge for the future is not so different from the challenge faced by Unitarians and Universalists one hundred years ago: to avoid any impingement on our freedom for religion, while at the same time building a greater community of faith—the church of the future, a community founded on liberal values but also on universalist principles. Together, the openness of liberal religion coupled with the encompassing theology of universalism provides a legacy sufficient to the challenge of a new age.

Put another way, there is more than merely a semantic difference between religious liberalism and liberal religion. Are we liberals who happen to gather in churches, or are we churchmen and -women who practice our religion according to liberal principles? Religious liberalism necessarily places the emphasis on the nominative, liberalism. When this happens we run the danger of displacing the myriad dimensions of our faith in favor of a single precept, the precept of freedom. Beyond the constrictions such would place upon the sweep of our religious concern, there is a further danger in this as well. As the twentieth-century Unitarian Universalist ethicist James Luther Adams writes,

Idolatry occurs when a social movement adopts as the center for loyalty an idol, a segment of reality torn away from the context of universality, an inflated, misplaced abstraction made into an absolute. Liberalism in its generalized form has been the chief critic of the idolatries of creedalism, of church or political authoritarianism, of nationalistic, racial, or sexual chauvinism; but in its specialized form it has generated a new idolatry, the idolatry of "possessive individualism."

Here Adams stands squarely in the tradition of Bellows and Brooks.

While freedom is the watchword of our faith, each of these witnesses reminds us that we must take that freedom seriously. For one thing, we choose to be free together, with all that this entails, rather than remaining free alone. For another, free to dismiss the answers others have given to life's essential questions, we are not free to dismiss the questions themselves. In every age, religion has addressed itself to questions of life and death, of origins and destinations, of living well in order that life may be redeemed by some purpose that even death cannot dispel. To ignore such questions would be to diminish our humanity. It would strip our faith of depth.

It is up to us. We have so much to offer, so much to give, if only we might muster the courage and will to extend ourselves, to build our institutions, to give our faith the breadth and scope that it deserves. To those who choose to follow, we have something new to offer, something new of value. And much that is old, whatever is of value there as well. That which inspires us; that which gives us strength. Whatever is of beauty, whatever brings to our world joy and to our lives the will to give of ourselves to the limit of our promise. This is what our liberal faith is all about. Not a rejection of religion, not a substitute for religion, but our own religion, that part of us, of our very being, that reckons face to face with life's eternal questions, that struggles and celebrates daily in search for purpose and meaning in life. Nothing cheap about it. Nothing shallow, unless we make it so. Unless we sell it short.

And we *are* responsible. That is one special thing about our liberal faith. Free to believe what we will, we are responsible for believing what we can. No one else is going to do it for us. Looked at in this way, there is no more serious, challenging, or compelling religion than this faith of ours. We are free. We are free to pitch ourselves into the very midst of life's teeming questions with all of our heart and mind and soul. We are free to redeem from death life's purpose. We are free to build and nurture a community of faith as stewards of the visible church, who carry its message in our lives.

CHAPTER 18

Universalism for the
Twenty-first Century

*I summed up the universalist theology underpinning my Unitarian Uni-
versalist faith in a major address delivered at our denomination's General
Assembly in 2001. Addressed specifically to my fellow Unitarian Universalists and intended as both a warning and an inspiration, it remains among
my most comprehensive theological statements and closes with a reprise and
deepening of my guiding metaphor, the Cathedral of the World.*

Three weeks before he died, my father chose the words for his tombstone. He weighed what message to post for strangers who might visit
his neighborhood some century hence. When we wander through
graveyards, we weigh our own mortality, so the "final instructions"
Frank Church left for future generations to ponder are humble
words, yet more than worthy of the splendid stone into which we
carved them:

> I never knew [anyone] who felt self-important in the morning
> after spending the night in the open on an Idaho mountainside
> under a star-studded summer sky.

Don't forget to spend some time in nature,
where you can bear witness to the wonder of God.

I never thought of my father as a religious man. He quit the Catholic Church when he was fourteen. I sensed that for him the Catholic Church was the one true church; it just happened to be false. Yet the words on my father's tombstone witness eloquently to the humble yet awestruck universalist spirit. By definition, universalism is not the province of any one sect. Humility and awe, two essential handmaidens for a heartfelt universalism, lie at the root of all direct human experience of the holy.

The word "human" has a telling etymology, my very favorite. All the words that relate to it are illuminating: humane, humanitarian, humility, humble, and, finally, humus. From dust to dust, we live and move and have our being. Our kinship is a mortal kinship. Though the human pilgrimage may wind down a million paths, all roads alike lead to the grave. In the temple of universalism, two great pillars—awe and humility—flank the doors. The doors themselves are birth and death.

We Unitarian Universalists have inherited a magnificent theological legacy. In a sweeping answer to dogmas that divide the human family, Unitarianism proclaims that we spring from a single source; Universalism, that we share a common destiny. That we are brothers and sisters by nature, our Unitarian and especially our Universalist forebears affirmed as a matter of faith: Unitarianism by positing a single God, Universalism by offering the promise of shared salvation.

In its original expression, as a development within Christian theology, Universalism advanced the radical notion that all of God's children go to heaven. Interpreted more broadly, universalism is an inclusive faith, rejecting the divisive notion that people fit into two separate categories: sheep and goats, the saved and the damned. To help shape a contemporary universalism, I shall invoke the spirit, not the letter, of our Universalist forebears.

I don't disbelieve in an afterlife; I simply have yet to experience an afterlife, and therefore have little to say concerning one. All I know is this. First, nothing (including any imaginable afterlife) could be more amazing than life itself. Second, life as we know it is impossible without death. And finally, though theology may begin at the tomb's door—the specter of death prompts reflection on what life means—surely no revelation is more compelling or worth pondering than that of a newborn child emerging from its mother's womb. When "doing theology" I try to remember my father's advice. Theologians are wise to close their learned tomes at times and reopen the book of nature. Theology is a human construct. It begins with the miracle of our own existence. If awe and humility are universalism's principal handmaidens, beyond every other distinction birth, love, and death remain the sacraments that unite us in a shared, all-saving mystery.

With this life-affirming legacy comes an attendant responsibility, especially today on an ever more intimate planet where togetherness is no longer a luxury but a necessity. Yet even as we are thrown together by realities that shape our common destiny, centrifugal forces spin us faster and farther from each other, fracturing the one world we now experience and jeopardizing our common welfare. By retrenching in old, familiar ground, many religions offer a temporary, idealized refuge from this reality. To contend with the forces of fractionalization, a twenty-first-century theology requires nothing less than a new burst of universalism.

Two obstacles thwart fulfillment of this mission. First, universalism is an exacting gospel. Taken seriously, no theology is more challenging—morally, spiritually, or intellectually: to love your enemy as yourself; to view your tears in another's eyes; to respect and even embrace otherness, rather than merely to tolerate (literally, to "put up with") or, even worse, dismiss it.

None of this comes naturally. We are weaned on the rational presumption that if two people disagree, only one can be right. This formula works better in mathematics than it does in theology. Universalism reminds us of that truth. Yet even to approximate the universalist ideal remains devilishly difficult in actual practice. Given the natural human tendency toward division, universalists run the constant temptation to backslide in their faith. One can lapse and become a bad or lazy universalist as effortlessly as others become once-a-month Methodists or nominal Catholics.

The second obstacle is intrinsic to Unitarian Universalism itself. Though named after two doctrines, ours is a nondoctrinal faith. By definition, we don't even have to believe in our own name. We can be free from, for, or against whatever we choose. We should be thankful for that. But we also must remember that only a respect for the potential worth and dignity of every human being and a shared commitment to the interdependent web of being—each among Unitarian Universalism's guiding principles—present a saving alternative to the perils of internecine division in an ever more fractious world.

Given our commitment to pluralism, Unitarian Universalism should represent the perfect laboratory for modeling amity in a world rife with passions that stem from differences of belief. Often, however, we, too, muster more passion for that which divides than we do for all that unites us. We must ask ourselves this: If, in our communities of faith, we find it difficult to unite under the banner of one overarching sympathy, how can we hope to counter right-wing fundamentalists? Without a uniting passion of our own, without a deep, shared commitment to our own first principles, how can we presume to contest theologies that divide, not unite, the human family? Before pronouncing our fidelity to universalism, we must take our own theological inventory.

Although the limits and intrinsic wonder of human nature may recommend universalism as the most overarching and inclusive approach to theology, our many differences in human nurture mitigate against it. Since the questions we ask of creation are life-and-death questions, our answers are emotionally charged. It is hard to accept that, if we are right, those who differ can be anything but wrong. In this respect, many contemporary Unitarian Universalists are as culpable as our more orthodox cousins. We, too, forget that we are more alike in our ignorance than we differ in our knowledge.

In the United States, Unitarianism and Universalism grew out of the Protestant tradition. The theologian Paul Tillich defined the "Protestant principle" this way: "The first word of religion must be spoken against religion." This principle serves us well in the necessary work of reforming corrupt religious institutions. Nonetheless, it is primarily negative, not affirmative. One need only contrast Catholic and Protestant church history to perceive that Protestants are forever cutting themselves into pieces like cells dividing, each division in the name of evolution toward the cause of higher life. Theologically, the universalist principle is precisely the opposite: to unite the many into one.

A century and a half ago, observing the sectarian and spiritually pallid corrosion of a recently minted Unitarianism, my predecessor in the All Souls pulpit the Reverend Henry Whitney Bellows called for a new, more catholic church, one animated by the spirit of union rather than the eccentricities of individualism. He published this call in his great address, "The Suspense of Faith." As you can imagine, his choice of the word "catholic" raised more than a few Unitarian hackles. Yet Bellows was attempting only to call us home to a larger residence. He, too, was proclaiming a new universalism—a more inclusive, more affirmative, less Protestant faith.

In recent years Unitarian Universalism, after the two liberal churches joined together in a catholic act, of sorts, has remained riven by the Protestant temptation to divide. In fascinating rotation, one group or another among us has attempted to purify itself from possible contagion by distancing itself from the whole. To resist this temptation, we must beat our Protestant swords into universalist plowshares.

I know this will prove daunting. After all, by embracing the Protestant principle in its purest form, ever since the Reformation we on the far-left wing of the reform movement have been conducting a theological search-and-destroy mission. The goal has been to strip away the trappings of religion in an attempt to restore to faith its intellectual and spiritual integrity. This has been a noble and often salutary effort. But when all is said and done, it remains a little like trying to find the seed of an onion by peeling away its layers. Eventually, nothing is left but our tears.

In Unitarian circles, the Protestant principle manifested itself in the creation of modern gnostic, or knowledge-based, religious movements, from Christian Science in the nineteenth century to some of today's New Age conventicles. It also periodically prompts calls for a retrenchment in eighteenth-century deism or early-twentieth-century modernism. Yet in almost every instance, regardless of expression or form, Unitarian implementation of the Protestant principle comes wrapped in the guise of rationalism. In marked contrast, Universalism, and indeed Unitarian transcendentalism, holds that by sheer rationality alone we cannot come close to comprehending the mystery of being alive and having to die. Life is a miracle that can't be explained without explaining it away. Our most profound encounters lead inexorably from the rational to the transrational realm.

Many leading scientists are ahead of us in this regard. Some recent discoveries in physics and cosmology make no apparent sense according to known canons of rationality. Probing the mysteries of the universe and the mind, researchers on the cutting edge of knowledge find themselves moving freely between the rational and transrational realms. Where does that leave the poor camp followers, who believe in science but don't embrace mystery? Having traded God for truth, they are left with neither.

Reason and rationality are entirely different things. Drawing from experience, reason dares us to imagine beyond what mere rationality excludes. Rationality excludes only the irrational. There is gain in this exclusion, for much religion today continues to be irrational. That is to say, it bases its rational claims on the evidence of a privileged revelation. Claims of scriptural inerrancy, virgin birth, and creation science start with the scriptures, not the cosmos, and in so doing limit rational activity to so closed a circle as to be indeed irrational. But an equally serious charge can be leveled at rational religion, especially in its most radical, almost always reactionary, form. In a principled flight from irrationality, rationalists betray reason by losing sight of the transrational realm, where rationalism is not rejected but transcended. This is the realm of myth and parable, of poetry and paradox. Wholeness cannot be achieved until we explore the two realms—of sign and symbol, fact and fancy—as one.

The danger of excluding the transrational from our field of contemplation is that, by sophisticating our minds against the mystery of powers so beyond our control and understanding as to be unimaginable, we lose our sense of humility and awe. We take the creation for granted, rather than receiving it with fitting gratitude as an undeserved, unfathomable gift. When rationalism supplants mystery, our imagination and sense of wonder are as likely to die as the gods we pride ourselves for having killed.

I confess to having participated in this slaughter myself. At the very outset of my ministry, I found greater confirmation for my own beliefs in Thomas Jefferson's rational unitarianism than in Ralph Waldo Emerson's mystical universalism. I believed most avidly in that which I could parse and thereby comprehend. The ethics of Jesus moved me; the Oversoul did not.

Over the years, I have slowly discovered that the self-confident posture of Enlightenment philosophy did not serve me as well as it appears to have served Jefferson. Jefferson and the French philosophes who inspired him brought God home by clipping God's wings, by domesticating mystery and caging it. To give my universalism full play, I had to make room in my theology for a more capacious, if unfathomable, power. I had to clear a place for mystery on the altar of my hearth, which before I had crowded with icons to knowledge. As a parish minister, this should have come naturally, but at first it didn't. In some respects, I knew religion too well to be anything but suspicious of its answers. God is on the label of every bottle of religious snake oil I have ever tasted. Before I could animate my own universalism, I therefore had to reimagine God.

It is impossible to speak of universalism without addressing the subject of God. Early Universalists believed that everyone was born to be saved because God was too good to damn them. To practice and proclaim a twenty-first-century universalism, we need not believe in the old Universalist God—we don't even have to employ the word "God"—but we must have an equally affectionate relationship with the ground of our being. Otherwise, we will succumb to the temptation to divide it between our own and others' feet.

Far better to seek common ground, beginning with the one miracle we all share. We exist because the universe was pregnant with us when it was born. In miracle and fact, our gestation traces to the beginning of time. Accidents abound, of course. One amino lapse or missed coupling and we would not be in the position to wonder why we are here. Yet, in my experience, only by positing the existence of a power beyond our comprehension can we begin to account for the miracle of being with an appropriate measure of humility and awe.

I recognize that for many people the word "God" has shrunk from repeated use, but we can always stretch it again. If you can't manage to do this—the G-word fitting your mind more like a straitjacket than a divine garment—then simply substitute another. "Spirit" may work for you, "the sacred" or "the holy" or "higher power." As long as the object of your reverence is large enough, it doesn't really matter, not at all.

I will say, however, that a new universalism may be ill served by the creation of a more private and thereby exclusive theological vocabulary. In a country where more than 90 percent of the people claim to believe in God, it may prove easier to inculcate faith in a larger God than to displace familiar affections. This aside, there is nothing novel, and certainly nothing blasphemous, about redesigning or renaming God. Responding to life-and-death questions, seekers have reinvented and thereby rediscovered the holy throughout the centuries.

Framing these questions, for scientist and theologian alike, our common text is the creation. Though limited by the depth and field of our vision, we are driven to make sense of it as best we can. So we tell stories, formulate hypotheses, develop schools of thought and worship, and pass our partial wisdom down from generation to generation. Interpreters with differing approaches, methodologies, and tools struggle to discover who we are, where we have come from, how we got here, and where we are heading and why and how. Each works from a set of basic presuppositions. Each has its trusted tools, such as the Bible or the Hubble telescope. As among literary critics, there is a continuing discussion within each school and occasional dialogue between them. Religions adapt to new discoveries in science. Scientists sometimes reach the point of farthest penetration and adopt the mystical language of reverence and adoration. The stakes are high. Of all intellectual contests, none is more charged or dangerous. Each side reckons the score in a different fashion, and there is no mutually accepted guideline for who is winning, even for how to play. Viewed as competition, the only way to secure a final victory is to discount or eliminate one's opponents.

And yet, if there can be many arguable interpretations of a poem, what should this tell us about the cosmos itself? Nothing is more mysterious or more veiled than the secret of the cosmos. No dogma can begin to comprehend it. Even as a scientific investigator cannot measure the velocity and position of a particle at the same time, the moment we begin to parse the creation we change its apparent nature. Gestalt psychology suggests a like point in object and field studies, for instance that well-known optical illusion of two faces in profile that also outline the shape of a vase. It is possible to go back and forth from one focus to another, but—though both are before our very eyes—we can't see the faces and the vase at once. In each instance, the investigator becomes part of the experiment, affecting the very data he or she is attempting objectively to collect. Not only are we the interpreters of God's poetry, we participate in the poem we ponder.

This doesn't mean that the search for truth or knowledge is in vain. In fact, discoveries such as Heisenberg's uncertainty principle (pointing out that the experimenter affects the data) are breakthroughs in knowledge. Nor does it mean that all truths are relative and therefore functionally interchangeable, only that no truth within the compass of human knowledge is absolute or final. The fact that ultimate truth is not privileged to any one particular religious, philosophical, or scientific system in no way rules out the possible existence of such a truth (or God). It simply underscores the natural limits of every human truth claim.

That there are innumerable ways to interpret the masterpiece of creation is a universalist touchstone, indeed our guiding principle: to affirm the discrete beauty of many windows even as unitarianism (as a doctrine, not a sect) proclaims the one light. Which invites us to return to the Cathedral of the World, and examine the windows and light a little more closely.

Universalism, as encapsulated in my cathedral metaphor, can be perverted in two ways. One is to elevate one truth into a universal truth: "My church is the one true church." The other is to reduce distinctive truths to a lowest common denominator: "All religion is merely a set of variations on the golden rule." The universalism I embrace does neither. In the Cathedral of the World, the same light shines through all our windows, but each window is different. The windows modify the light, refracting it in various patterns that suggest discrete meanings. Just as one cannot believe in "everything," to find meaningful expression universalism must be modified or refracted through the glass of individual and group experience (which by definition is less than universal).

By pondering the light through a Christian window, one can be a Christian Universalist, or, respectively, a Jewish, Buddhist, Muslim, or Hindu Universalist. One cannot, however, according to this model, be a Universalist Christian (Hindu, Muslim, Buddhist, or Jew). Rather than modifying the whole by the part, thereby offering focus, one would instead be elevating the part above the whole, with the encompassing adjective, "universalist," subsumed under the more narrow theological claims it modifies.

Religion is dangerous, especially today, on a shrinking globe where conflicting faith positions contest one another in almost every human precinct. Yet every generation has had its holy warriors, hard-bitten zealots for whom the world is large enough for only one true faith. Tightly drawn, their logic makes a demonic kind of sense:

1. Religious answers respond to life-and-death questions, which happen to be the most important questions of all.
2. You and I may come up with different answers.
3. If you are right, I must be wrong.
4. I can't be wrong, because my salvation hinges on my being right.
5. Therefore, you must be wrong.

Aristotle coined something called the law of the excluded middle. As a logical certainty, he asserted that A and *not A* cannot both be true at one and the same time. By the light of my cathedral metaphor,

Aristotle was mistaken, at least with respect to theology. His logical certitude oversteps the law of experience. Contrast one stained-glass window (its dark center bordered by more translucent panes) with another (configured in the opposite fashion). Though the same light shines through both, they will cast diametrically opposite shadow images on the cathedral floor (*A* and *not A*, if you will). Is the truth darkness surrounded by light or light surrounded by darkness? In the Cathedral of the World, the answer is "both."

As refracted through the windows of tradition and experience, truth emerges indirectly. To a modern universalist, this suggests that—since the same light can be refracted in many different ways (including *A* and *not A*)—the only religious truth claims we can discount completely are those that dismiss all other claims for failing to conform to their own understanding of the creation.

One presumably impartial response to the war of theological passions is to reject religion, to distance ourselves from those who attempt, always imperfectly, to interpret the light's meaning. There are two problems with this approach. One is that it deprives us of a potentially deep encounter with the mysterious forces that impel our being, thereby limiting our ability to invent and discover meaning. The second is that few of us actually are able to resist interpreting the light. Whether we choose the windows that enlighten existence for us or inherit them, for each individual the light and darkness mingle more or less persuasively as refracted through one set of windows or another. Attracted to the partial clarification of reality that emerges in patterns of light and the play of shadows, even people who reject religion are worshippers of truth as they perceive it. Their windows, too, become shrines.

Because none of us is able fully to comprehend the truth that shines through another person's window, nor to apprehend the falsehood that we ourselves may perceive as truth, we can easily mistake another's good for evil, and our own evil for good. Modern universalist theology tempers the consequences of our inevitable ignorance while addressing the overarching crisis of our times: dogmatic division in an ever more intimate, fractious, and yet interdependent world. It posits the following fundamental principles:

1. There is one power, one truth, one God, one light.
2. This light shines through every window in the cathedral.
3. No one can perceive it directly, the source of the mystery being forever veiled.
4. Yet, on the cathedral floor and in the eyes of each beholder, refracted and reflected here are patterns that suggest meanings, challenging us to interpret and live by these meanings as best we can.
5. Each window illumines truth in a unique way, leading to various truths, and these in differing measure according to the insight, receptivity, and behavior of the beholder.

This final point is essential. Unless some criterion exists to test the validity of one's truth claims, universalism lapses quickly into uncritical relativism. The criterion is this: our degree of enlightenment reflects itself not in our faith claims but in our lives. In a universalist construct, good behavior unites and heals; bad behavior destroys and divides. Unless our faith, whatever its particulars may be, helps us heal our lives (leading to integrity and a clear conscience), inspires us to reconcile with our neighbors (leading to peace), and plants our feet firmly on the ground of our being (uniting us with the one light, truth, or God), we have been blinded by the light that shines through our chosen window, unaware of the long shadow that those who bathe themselves blindly in the light can cast.

Fortunately, since the light shines through each window, as we ponder and act on insights derived from even a single reflection, we may instead find illumination. In the Cathedral of the World, we can discover or invent meanings that invest both the creation and our lives with greater purpose. Having been healed ourselves, we can help heal the world. And when we do, we will open our hearts to a song of universal praise.

CHAPTER 19

Emerson's Shadow

In the third volume of his magisterial history of American liberal theol-ogy (The Making of American Liberal Theology: Crisis, Irony, & Postmodernity, 1950–2005*), Gary Dorrien titles the section devoted to my theology "Recovering Transcendentalist Universalism." I had traced the roots of my theology to Paul Tillich—I do so, for instance, in my book* The Essential Tillich. *On further reflection I think Dorrien has slotted me correctly. The font I discovered in Emersonian transcendentalism has certainly defined and deepened my faith. Where I differ from Emerson, and differ profoundly, is in his emphasis on self-reliance, an emphasis that has gone a great distance to shape the American character. Emerson's sovereign indi-vidualism and patent lack of human sympathy constitute a negative print image of my universalist theology. Later in this section, I shall offer a paean to Emerson and how his theology has inspired me. Here I explore the dark side of this archetypal American thinker's otherwise luminous moon.*

Ralph Waldo Emerson memorably said, "Every institution is the lengthened shadow of one man." Unitarian Universalism is too multidimensional to fit neatly within a single shadow, but if any re-flection were protean enough to encompass us it would certainly be Emerson's. Free-spirited, iconoclastic, and self-actualizing, the Sage

of Concord—more sage than the Boston Unitarians of his own day—
is the true father of our faith.

Two hundred years have passed since Waldo was born into the
family of a prominent Unitarian minister. After following his father
into the ministry for a brief tenure at Boston's Second Church, in
quick succession he left first his pastorate, then preaching, and finally the church altogether (only to return in his dotage). Yet today,
having completely recovered from Emerson's rejection, Unitarian
Universalism positively basks in his reflected aura. Roof to pillar, all
manner of things Unitarian Universalist, from churches to UUA
donor-recognition circles, boast his name. Theologically as well,
Emerson continues to shape and enliven the faith he once so eloquently scorned. As do many of our ministers, I turn to him often for
theological guidance and spiritual illumination.

Beyond the ironies implicit here, there is also a shadow side to
Emerson's influence. To whatever extent organized Unitarian Universalism represents "the lengthened shadow of one man," it lan-
guishes in that shadow. Emerson's shadow blocks us from becoming
who we might be, should we ever decide to grow up.

Emerson was the quintessential adolescent sage. I don't mean that
pejoratively. Adolescence, the passage from childish dependence to
maturity, is no less necessary a stage for a nation or a faith than for an
individual. Coming of age together, Emerson, the United States, and
the Unitarian movement shared the same adolescent passage. Newly
liberated from England, the nation was a child when Emerson was
born in 1803. The American Unitarian Association was formed in
1825, when Emerson was studying for the ministry. Quickly thereafter, freethinkers in the movement began to challenge every lingering
assumption tying young Unitarianism to its Christian parentage.

Emerson chafed at all forms of servitude, dedicating his full intellectual energy to the liberation of American letters from outworn
and derivative Old World models. "Our day of dependence, our long
apprenticeship to the learning of other lands, draws to a close," he
wrote in his personal declaration of independence, "The American
Scholar."

From the publication of *Nature* in 1836 until his death in 1882, no figure—political, literary, or religious—better kindled the adolescent spirit necessary for a young people to stand on its own feet and chart a course independent from that of their elders.

Yet, to be functional, adolescence must be age-appropriate. If Emerson's philosophy spoke to his own times, in the meantime one might hope that our nation and faith have matured. In developmental theory the progression goes as follows: dependence, independence, interdependence. In an age of bondlessness, Emerson's script (sovereign individualism and self-reliance) does not address today's need for interdependence. This holds true for nation and denomination both. If we are ever to grow up, the anti-institutionalists who gravitate to our institutions must take a little of their precious Emersonian freedom and invest it more generously. Only then will we bond together in redemptive community. Until we, as Unitarian Universalists, come out from under Emerson's shadow, we will not mature as a movement.

To build an institution on a foundation laid by an anti-institutionalist is a little like hiring a demolition expert as one's architect. Emerson left his parish over a disagreement with the entire standing committee of the Second Church over his refusal to perform the sacrament of communion. To a majority of modern Unitarian Universalists, this confirms his reputation as a prophet. But Emerson's rebellion against the church went much deeper. To begin with, his shyness and aversion to intimacy made him temperamentally unsuited to the pastorate. "It has many duties for which I am feebly qualified," he confessed to his congregation. More importantly, he came to view the church as a mausoleum. "I like the silent church before the service begins, better than any preaching," Emerson said. Could he say as much for the silent lyceum before he began his lecture?

If one were to pick a word to describe Ralph Waldo Emerson, it would be "counterdependent." "Friend, client, child, sickness, fear, want, charity, all knock at once at thy closet door and say, 'Come out to us,'" he complained. "But keep thy state; come not into their confusion." Believing that people "descend to meet" and that "nothing can bring you peace but yourself," this gentle Platonist was adamantine in his diffidence. Lacking empathetic imagination, he considered sympathy "base." "No man can come near me but through my act," he said.

All these quotes are from Emerson's most abidingly influential essay, "Self-Reliance," published in 1841, a relentless screed against every manner of conformity to the "profane" expectations of society. "Self-help" (a term that he was among the first to employ) was Emerson's watchword. As reported by his grandson, Emerson often admitted, "My strength and my doom is to be solitary." He reveled in his strength and doom. "Leave me alone and I should relish every hour and what it brought me," he wrote in "Experience." But in the same essay he was also pensive: "I grieve that grief can teach me nothing." Years before, at the age of nineteen, he had pegged himself perfectly: "I have not the kind affections of a pigeon."

"Profane" was Emerson's favorite epithet. He applied it to his own person, if not to his essential self. In 1841 he confided in his journal, "These hands, this body, this history are profane and wearisome, but I, I descend not to mix myself with that or with any man." In those rare moments of self-assessment that punctuate his litanies of divine elevation, Emerson lamented his emotional austerity, especially the toll it took on those closest to him. Accounting truth "handsomer than the affection of love," he nonetheless appears to have craved the affection he spurned in subordination to his higher goal. But never for long. "The great man," he reminded himself in "Compensation," "must always outrun that sympathy which gives him such satisfaction.... He must hate father and mother, wife and child."

From all accounts, during the ten-month separation from his family when Emerson took his second tour of Europe in 1847, his long-suffering wife, Lydia, knew unaccustomed health and joy in the chaste company of Henry David Thoreau. Even then, she longed for Emerson's withheld affection. "You still ask me for that unwritten letter always due, always unwritten, from year to year, by me to you," he wrote his wife from England. Unable to honor his wife's request for a simple declaration of love, Emerson responded to her cry for sympathy by indulging in his own pathos: "I truly acknowledge a poverty of nature, and have really no proud defense to set up, but ill-health, puniness, and Stygian limitations."

Emerson's aversion to human intimacy did not prevent him from idealizing (almost idolizing) friendship. And what friends he had. His otherworldly wisdom, coupled with a serene temperament, were magnets to a dozen or more brilliant companions. Throughout much of their adult lives Thoreau, Margaret Fuller, and Bronson Alcott each sought his friendship and approval. He was especially drawn to insouciant young poets like Ellery Channing and Jones Very. To Emerson, the ideal community was a company of two like-minded spirits, master and pupil, walking together, ideally in silence, through the woods.

Yet Emerson's belief that "every man alone is sincere; at the entrance of a second person, hypocrisy begins," put a strain on even his closest relations. Due to his intolerance of imperfection, Emerson's friendships were phosphorescent—spontaneously illuminating and as quickly extinguished by his aversion to intimacy. Poised to retreat at the slightest sign of entanglement, he kept his friends (alternatively ecstatic at his attentions and disappointed by their removal) at arm's length.

Pure in his idealism, Emerson met disappointment in his friendships. "All association must be a compromise," he pined. In his essay "Circles," Emerson summed up his regrets about the chosen few in whom he serially invested and withheld intimacy. "Men cease to interest us when we find their limitations. The only sin is limitation. As soon as you once come up with a man's limitation, it is all over with him."

Given his nature, it is not surprising that Emerson stood aloof—despite his liberal social sympathies—from those who were attempting to reform society. Describing Sunday schools, churches, and charitable associations as "yokes to the neck," he was especially barbed in his dismissal of Unitarians. In "The Sovereignty of Ethics"—displaying a rare flash of humor—he speculated, "Luther would cut his hand off sooner than write theses against the pope if he suspected that he was bringing on with all his might the pale negations of Boston Unitarianism." Unitarian Universalists who today might join him, as I do, in rejecting the spiritual aridity and constrictive rationalism early dominant in the mother church, should not rejoice prematurely in their kinship with Emerson. "Your miscellaneous popular charities;" he wrote in "Self-Reliance," "the education at college of fools; the building of meeting houses to the vain end to which many now stand; alms to sots, and the thousand-fold Relief Societies; though I confess with shame I sometimes succumb and give the dollar, it is a wicked dollar, which by and by I shall have the manhood to withhold." On this foundation one cannot build a church.

Emerson espoused the libertarian belief that self-reliance, if practiced widely, would alone solve most of the world's problems. He was an early supply-sider, an advocate of trickle-down compassion. "Let the amelioration in our laws of property proceed from the concession of the rich, not from the grasping of the poor," he wrote in "Man the Reformer." Emerson embraced the ideal of reform, but found the petulance of reformers distasteful. With the singular exception of emancipation (for which he occasionally and eloquently came down briefly from his aerie to expound), Emerson's fastidious code of conduct precluded sullying himself in the company of those who were working to ameliorate the plight of the poor, extend human dignity, or advocate temperance. Reform is "done profanely, not piously; by management, by tactics and clamor," he primly complained in his "Introductory Lecture on the Times." "It is a buzz in the ear. I cannot feel any pleasure in sacrifices which display to me such partiality of character." In the garden of his times, Emerson was a sensitivity plant. Brush rudely up against him and he would instantly recoil.

The closest Emerson comes to a comprehensive self-critique is in "The Transcendentalist," his essay on the loose school of New England nature mystics that many credit him with founding. Describing his fellow transcendentalists as "exacting children," he summed up the movement's adolescent limitations more succinctly than any critic. "So many promising youths, and never a finished man," he wrote. "They are not good citizens, not good members of society.... They do not willingly share in the public charities, in the public religious rites, in the enterprises of education, of missions foreign and domestic, in the abolition of the slave trade, or in the temperance society. They do not even like to vote." In defense of his fellow travelers' scruples, Emerson explains that all great causes seem "paltry matters" to them.

"On the part of these children it is replied that life and their faculty seem to them gifts too rich to be squandered on such trifles." Then, tellingly, he changes tense and speaks in the first person. "What am I? What but a thought of serenity and independence.... I do not wish to do one thing but once.... The path which the hero travels alone is the highway of health. I will not molest myself for you. I do not wish to be profaned.... I will not move until I have the highest command." Having had four adolescent children of my own and myself having excelled in adolescence beyond the years traditionally allotted to it, these sentiments could not be more familiar.

To mature as a faith, Unitarian Universalism must step out of Emerson's shadow. Paradoxically—and it is impossible to write about Emerson without invoking paradox—once we do this, the light that shined on him, illuminating his deepest thoughts, may brighten our own path. As he himself said of Virgil, Emerson "is a thousand books to a thousand persons." His books may trumpet sovereign individualism, but they are orchestrated with a harmonious spirituality. That spirit enhances our prospects for interdependence by fostering a reverence for all life. Of the Oversoul he wrote, "The heart of thee is in the heart of all."

As intimate with nature as he was guarded in his personal relations, Emerson is the poet laureate of the interdependent web of life. "Every chemical substance, every plant, every animal in its growth, teaches the unity of cause, the variety of appearance," he wrote in his essay "History." Speaking there of "the chain of affinity," and elsewhere (in "Compensation") perceiving that "the world globes itself in a drop of dew," Emerson was a vivid part of the poem he pondered. When walking through Concord on his daily stroll, he almost never failed to enter a field of enchantment. In his essay "Plato," Emerson expresses the essential oneness of creation by way of analogy: "The ploughman, the plough, and the furrow are of one stuff."

Here his pulse can quicken our own. Modern Unitarian Universalism is as captive to linear reasoning and the constrictions of rational positivism as Boston Unitarianism in Emerson's day was bound to the presumptuous logic of supernatural rationalism. Emerson's awe and cosmic humility can help us tune life's wondrous manifestations to "the miraculous hum of their spindle."

To be fair, Emerson sought no disciples. He wished no one to languish in his shadow any more than he himself was content to bathe in the reflected glory of his own heroes. What he asked of his own generation in *Nature*, he also asks of us: "Why should we not also enjoy an original relationship with the universe." Beyond this, however much it owes to his gospel of self-reliance, Emerson would recoil at the tyranny of modern American individualism. At the inertia and conformity we witness today, he would bridle with a rebellion appropriate to the sins of a new age. He might even cast down the idol of sovereign individualism he helped to erect.

But that is our work now. If we band together, cultivate interdependence, build strong institutions, support them generously, and become more fully accepting and embracing of one another, we, too, can extricate ourselves from the shadow of the past—in our case Emerson's shadow. We can come of age. Going one step further, by walking forward together with reverence and awe, we will honor this remarkable man's memory in a way that he would celebrate. We will honor it by emerging from Emerson's shadow into Emerson's light.

CHAPTER 20

There Is No Hell

Staging a debate in 2006 over whether or not hell exists, the folks at Beliefnet invited me to argue the negative. I do believe in hell on earth. But the notion of hell as a destination of eternal punishment designed by God to right the harmony of the universe leaves me absolutely cold. The Universalist denomination emerged in eighteenth-century America among people who no longer could believe in hell. In this piece, I reach back to affirm the stance boldly taken by my Universalist predecessors.

The difference between Universalists and Unitarians (the old joke has it) is that Universalists believe that God is too good to damn them, whereas Unitarians believe that they're too good to be damned. By that measure, I am a Universalist.

For all my many failings, the day I wake up dead I won't be in a cattle car on the fast train to Satan's fiery pit. Nor will you. And neither will Old Scratch himself. If he actually exists, the devil, too, will be saved—after, according to second-century universalist theologian Origen, a tempering intermission in purgatory. In the good news of universalism, God is a loving God who will not rest until the entire creation is redeemed. All creatures will be saved. There is no hell.

It's easy to understand why hell was invented (if quite late in the biblical record). Eternal damnation solves the sticky part of the problem of evil: why do good things happen to bad people? Reserving a corner of hell for all who escape well-deserved punishment here on earth balances the moral ledger sheet. Justice is done. Otherwise, not only is life unfair; the afterlife becomes unfair as well.

The problem is, when we project our retributive logic onto a cosmic screen, we pervert the divine image. We predicate hell on the irreverent presumption that God's appetite for vengeance (an all-voracious version of our own nagging hunger) must be satisfied. "She'll get hers in hell," we say. That balances our ledger, but it turns God into a jailer.

The idea of purgatory makes perfectly good sense. I can imagine the utility of corrective punishment. But eternal hellfire demeans everything I believe about God. As important, it eviscerates the heart of Jesus's gospel.

Jesus was anything but a biblical literalist. He teaches by parable, not by citing chapter and verse, and gets into holy mischief by repeatedly breaking the letter of scripture. Love is the sum and substance of all the law and the prophets, he teaches. He enjoins us to forgive and love our enemies. "Your enemy be damned" is no part of his gospel.

"Be perfect as your Father in Heaven is perfect," Jesus instructs his disciples. That perfection can be summed up in three words, each an expression of divine love: justice, mercy, and forgiveness. Standing alone, justice might allow for the creation of hell, but mercy and forgiveness render it morally impossible. We can sift a spoonful of evidence for hell from the scriptures, even as we can ladle out dozens of arguments for slavery. Neither, however, meets the requirements of the biblical spirit, whose imperative is love.

It's no wonder that hell is the watchword for religious terror. By tempting the fallen angels of our nature, the very idea of it undermines the principles of mercy and forgiveness. You don't have to be a terrorist to be crippled by the idea of hell, however. Couple "Not to worry, for God will punish her eternally" to the sound adage, "Hate the sin and love the sinner," and it becomes a noxious bromide.

It is impossible to hate a person and pray for him at the same time. Visualize in your mind someone who causes you profound pain.

Remind yourself that your enemy is a child of God. If that doesn't break the spell, remember (and not with a smirk on your face) that he too will die one day. Then do something truly godlike. Pray that before your enemy dies, he may experience a taste of true peace and happiness.

Loving our enemies demands sacrifice (a word that means "to render sacred"). We sacrifice self-righteousness, bitterness, and pride, knowing that such an act will cleanse our souls and make our lives right with all that is holy. At our most reverent, having resisted the temptation to damn our enemy to hell, we go one step further and pray for her immortal soul. We try to be perfect, as God in heaven is perfect.

If, following Jesus's lead, we open ourselves to the workings of grace when we forgive our enemies, how could God imaginably entertain a plan of selective redemption based on a retributive justice system with no possibility for parole? If we, mere humans, can unlock our hearts by praying for someone who has inflicted unforgettable damage on us, would God damn to eternal hellfire every creature who has failed life's course?

God may not actually be love—the mystery of creation is too deep for human equivalents to approximate—but we know from experience and the spirit of the scriptures that love is divine.

None of us is too good to be damned, but God is too good and too loving to damn us. There is no hell.

CHAPTER 21

The Seven Deadly Virtues

My first foray into theology was a trilogy of books I wrote in the late 1980s designed to "remythologize humanism." In The Devil & Dr. Church, Entertaining Angels, *and* The Seven Deadly Virtues, *I revisited hell, heaven, and purgatory to see if the rich traditional imagery of Christianity could be translated to serve the needs of liberal theology. In the third of these books, I introduced my vision of the Commonwealth of God. To enter, we had to overcome our so-called virtues as much as we needed to triumph over our sins. Potentially more deadly than our sins, our virtues invite us to elevate ourselves above others and, by so doing, lull us into complacency. Insulated by the feeling that all is right with us, we tend to overlook that all is not right with the world, and that as part of the world, we are part of everything that is wrong.*

Medievalist and mystery writer Dorothy Sayers defines the seven deadly virtues as "Respectability, Childishness, Mental Timidity, Dullness, Sentimentality, Censoriousness, Depression of Spirits." In truth, when ranking virtues according to toxicity, only one measurement need be taken. As Shakespeare reminds us, "Virtue itself turns vice, being misapplied." The more elevated the virtue, the more deadly. By this criterion, in the above collection of seven deadly vir-

143

tues only respectability and sentimentality come even close to passing muster.

Using this simple test to discriminate between venial and venal virtues (the former being those that have the capacity to poison us only a little), each of us would figure up a slightly different list no doubt. Albeit liberal in my leanings, being a traditionalist as well I shall avoid originality here. I am content to regard the seven traditional Christian virtues as the deadliest virtues of all. Divided into their customary groupings—the philosophical virtues (as codified by Plato) and the theological virtues (which were added by Gregory the Great in the sixth century)—the seven deadly virtues are as follows: prudence, justice, temperance, fortitude; and then faith, hope, and love.

If you were going to package American virtue in a box, you'd have to put Horatio Alger on the cover. The seven deadly virtues are bootstrap virtues. In Alger's stories, poor little boys filled with wile, pluck, and derring-do heroically prove that virtue is its own reward by employing faith, hope, prudence, temperance, and fortitude in order to clamber over their more privileged but less driven contemporaries to the top. If Horatio Alger's hero were growing up today and somehow managed not to end up as a Wall Street CEO or a hedge fund manager, you would probably find him on the real streets of America pushing drugs.

Until recently, when the roof caved in on the American economy, supply-side economists were fond of pointing out that a rising tide lifts all boats. But as the gap grows between rich and poor, which it has every year since 1980, it becomes clear that the rising tide they've been talking about has lifted only the yachts and the battleships; the rowboats got swamped in the wake. It's hardly surprising that a growing number of ambitious young men have chosen to trade in their rowboats for speedboats.

We are all insider traders, of course. At one time or another, we have successfully rationalized selling our souls for profit. No one is more sincere than a virtuous sinner. There is no shortage of lofty ends to justify whatever means we may chose to elevate our crimes to the status of nobility. But what's good for the goose is also bad for the goose, and may be devastating to the flock.

Evil is not the privation of good; it is the perversion of good. This is why our "virtues" are so dangerous, both collectively and to us as individuals. Any given quality or value, if lifted above the scale of associated values and weighed independently, becomes an evil.

This is true of all the virtues, even temperance. Adolf Hitler was a teetotaler and a vegetarian. This helped keep his mind and body pure. Hitler was devoted to purity. This same devotion, wildly misunderstood and misapplied, led him to commit genocide.

Sometimes the enemy is as evil as our representations make him or her out to be. Certainly this was true of Hitler. As sponsor of the Holocaust, a case study in evil disguised as good, here was a man more satanic than the most vicious caricature could ever portray. Yet, ironically, as the writer Kurt Vonnegut Jr. points out, "This was very bad for us.... Our enemies were so awful, so evil, that we, by contrast, must be remarkably pure. That illusion of purity, to which we were entitled in a way, has become our curse today." In the age of terrorism, we must remain especially alert to this temptation. Our most dangerous self-definition is the negative-print image. Its logic runs as follows: "Our enemies are evil. We are against them. Therefore we are good."

The Bible defines religion only in a handful of places, with Micah's definition perhaps the most inclusive: "And what does the Lord require of you," he asks, "but to do justice, love mercy, and walk humbly with your God." When the first two injunctions are in conflict, the third becomes essential.

By Micah's definition, when advocated with pride and not humility, militant ethics based on God's justice or even God's love are impious. They mask their own crime, a crime against the very virtue they pronounce. For instance, love of one country or ideology often expresses itself as fear of another, and fear leads us to hate. Even if the system we oppose is hateful, actions instructed by fear are likely to be more consonant with a hateful system of government than with a loving one. And with "eye for an eye" justice, both sides end up blind. Here, another of Micah's admonitions—"The best of us is like a briar; the most upright of us a thorn hedge.... Our confusion is at hand"—becomes not only figuratively but also literally true.

Think of the power that accompanies our new technologies. Today we possess both the powers of creation (with molecular cloning) and the powers of destruction (with the splitting of atoms). From Genesis to Revelation, from the alpha of creation to the omega of apocalypse, God's domain has become our own.

With knowledge continuing to outstrip wisdom, whether we can handle God's work is a highly doubtful proposition. But if we can't, there will be hell to pay.

Take the stories of Prometheus and Faust. Running parallel to the first chapters of Genesis, in the tale of Prometheus, Zeus made humankind out of clay. Relegated to a station little higher than the beasts, lacking all knowledge of the heavenly secrets and possessing only the most rudimentary tools, at first we posed no threat to God. But then Prometheus, half god, half man, stole fire from heaven, empowering us with technology to lift us beyond our bestial state. Zeus punished Prometheus by chaining him to a mountain crag, where an eagle daily fed on his liver, which was restored each succeeding night. Yet, with the gift of fire and other godlike powers of craft and art brought down from Olympus, Prometheus succeeded in liberating the human race from bondage to Zeus.

Contrast this tale with that of Dr. Faustus, the sixteenth-century German magician who is said to have, in exchange for knowledge and power, sold his soul to the devil. At first Faust was depicted as little more than a fool (in the original puppet plays) or charlatan (in Christopher Marlowe's *The Tragicall History of Dr. Faustus*). But over the years his legend underwent a telling metamorphosis. Throughout the Age of Reason, as our faith in science and technology grew, people began to see Faust's crime in a new light. Coupled in the nineteenth century with the romantic lionization of superheroes, men and women who dared to flout convention, this led to the resurrection of Faust as a modern hero, a natural protagonist. First the German dramatist Gotthold Lessing and then Lessing's countryman, Johann Wolfgang von Goethe, rewrote the Faust legend with a happy ending. Supplanting God's scruples, individual human genius augmented by power proved stronger than the devil. Faust won his wager and was saved.

Then follows the twentieth century: two world wars, the Holocaust, the atomic bomb. Destruction reigned as never before, translating from triumphant to tragic Faust's higher knowledge. In his novel *Doctor Faustus*, written just after World War II, Thomas Mann suggests that neither Lessing's principle of education nor Goethe's Hegelian synthesis is sufficient to rescue Faust from this new hell. Following in lockstep with the ravaging of Europe, tragic, brilliant, modern Dr. Faustus, feverishly burning, reaps what he and his century have sown.

Prometheus and Faust both seek powers hitherto denied to humankind, and both suffer as a result. But where Prometheus's suffering has meaning, Faust's does not. Dr. Faust sells his soul to the devil for his own selfish purposes. A modern-day gnostic, he seeks knowledge and mastery for their own sake, regardless of the consequences. Prometheus, in jeopardizing *his* future, does so not for himself but explicitly to guarantee a better future for humankind. In wresting control of divine powers that enhance our status in the great chain of being, each is playing with fire, Faust the fire of hell (which incinerates), Prometheus the fire of heaven (which purifies).

The universalist theologian Origen, who believed in purgatory but not in hell, was graphic in his description of the fires of judgment burning in purgatory. "This fire consumes not the creature, but what the creature has himself built....It is manifest that the fire destroys the wood of our transgressions, and then returns to us the reward of our good works."

Purgatory on earth is hell tempered by heaven, shadows of happiness, bright fields of desolation, both of which remind us that, despite our pain—in fact, because of it—we're already saved the moment we open our hearts, and therefore have saving work to do before we die. Unlike tattered desert or garret creatures, pilgrims in purgatory are not expatriates from the world. They are patriots of the Commonwealth of God.

When Aeschylus wrote *Prometheus Bound*, even when Marlowe wrote his *Dr. Faustus*, our world was divided—the heavens above, the earth below. We were the center of the universe, of God's attention, yet ever in danger of becoming estranged from God by thinking too much of ourselves. The old pattern of hubris and nemesis, presumption and fall, was understood in the context of a divided ground of spiritual being, ours and God's. Unsolicited trespass beyond our appointed territory invited swift destruction.

Two major shifts decisively alter our perspective. First, we are no longer the center of the universe. Not only does the sun not revolve around the earth, but the sun itself is a lesser sun in the great scheme of things, a peripheral star. The other shift is that, even as we recognize ourselves to have receded in cosmic importance, we continue to augment our human powers to such an extent that powers once considered the unique prerogative of God, creation and apocalypse, are now within our human grasp.

Given the knowledge of good and evil, if like Faust we continue to use that knowledge for selfish, shortsighted, and narrow purposes, our hubris will lead to a nemesis of ultimate proportions. But if, like Prometheus, we share our warmth and light, then the fires we kindle will burn to bless and keep our world like beacons of true hope, guiding our fellow travelers through the dark yet luminous purgatorial night.

CHAPTER 22

Home After Dark

Reflecting more personally than ever before on the dual reality of being alive and having to die, I find myself asking, in face of death, what comfort does universalism offer? Is universalist theology intimate enough to embrace each individual as he or she walks through the valley of the shadow? Does a theology grounded in God's goodness contain sufficient grit to get us through times of crisis and trial? In closing this section, I weigh these questions in the balance of my theology, offering in this chapter and the next excerpts from my theological travelogue, Bringing God Home: A Spiritual Guidebook for the Journey of Your Life.

A quarter of a century ago in the middle of his thirty-third year, lying one cold winter morning in the darkness, Protestant theologian and psychologist James Fowler awakened fully and suddenly to the fact that he was going to die. In the introduction to his book, *The Stages of Faith*, Fowler writes that for the first time he saw mortality clearly: "This body, this mind, this lived and living myth, this husband, father, teacher, son, friend will cease to be. The tide of life that propels me with such force will cease and I—this *I* taken so much for granted by *me*—will no longer walk this earth." At first he felt frozen by a feeling of remoteness, from the room itself and from his wife sleeping in the bed beside him. As his many little triumphs and accomplishments raced through his mind, each felt vaporous and fictive. His faith as a Christian minister, too, seemed to have no real substance, appearing to him as shapeless as an overcoat hanging on the door of his room. Fowler got out of bed. "I seemed to stand completely naked—a soul without body, raiment, relationships or roles. A soul alone with—with what? With whom?"

Reflecting that faith is like an overcoat covering our nakedness, Fowler sought first to recover himself and then better to understand the many differing ways faith connects us to God. Sparked by a night of existential anguish, Fowler's search not only led to a rekindling of hope, but also—as is evident from his book—it invested his work with new-felt purpose. "Hope means to keep humming in the dark," wrote Fowler's contemporary, Catholic theologian Henri Nouwen. Such humming is by no means futile. As Fowler's experience suggests, the music of hope can harmonize the darkness. Life can lift its song from death's score.

Nothing tests our spiritual mettle like a proverbial dark night of the soul. Whatever casts us into the abyss—whether the specter of our own death, some self-inflicted agony, or a twist of fate—the journey through midnight toward morning can be excruciating. Yet it carries a gift. Much as the consciousness of being alive is enhanced by a heightened sense of death, our awareness of needing to be saved springs most surely from the experience of being lost.

My own dark nights descend sometimes without warning, often with unwelcome news their harbinger. I endure them in the usual way. After an initial bout of denial, arguing, and bargaining, I reconcile myself to whatever reality has visited upon me. Less tractable is the trouble I bring down on myself. The cost to our sense of well-being is particularly steep when its bill of particulars is a lengthy self-indictment of all the things that we might have done to avoid harming our own or others' lives. When we ourselves are to blame, time stops at midnight. Our minds haunt us with things that we can't change, words we can never take back, and deeds that are fixed in the record of our days. As one young woman in the All Souls church school put it, "Life doesn't come equipped with erasers."

A saving paradox is at work here, however. Spiritual opportunity visits more readily when we in fact *are* responsible for getting into the thicket through which we find ourselves wandering. About another's actions we can do little. But if we own our culpability (admittedly a big "if"), we may discover that we hold it in our power, if not to retrace our steps, at least to proceed in a new direction. If life doesn't come with erasers, we can always resharpen its point.

Though we alone may be responsible for our predicament, to escape the grip of self-imposed agony, we may need outside assistance. Don't think of this as weakness or as a crutch. When we fall, it takes more courage to ask for another's hand than it does to attempt lifting ourselves up by broken bootstraps. I was reminded again of this one spring, when—unexpectedly, almost miraculously—the book closed on an unfinished chapter of my life.

Years earlier, I had discovered the following letter under my study door.

Dear Mr. Church,

What is the meaning of adversity? I don't think I can handle it anymore. Nothing it seems has gone right in my life. I am very tired of this stupid life. If you can tell me the reason for suffering or pain or adversity, please tell me. I know people do not have an answer, and I know many people overcome adversity but I am tired of it. I feel absolutely hopeless. Is there a god or is there not a god? If I feel there is not a god what is the sense of going on? And for whom?

I know this letter sounds crazy, but I am tired of it. I feel absolutely hopeless.

—A Parishioner

P.S. Yes, I've had therapy and medication—now you must really think I'm crazy—but I remain hopeless. Please help me.

How could I be of help? I knew nothing about this person. Asking my staff for assistance, together we tossed around a few possible names. One sometime parishioner had just lost his wife and children to a tragic accident. Perhaps he was the one. Another was facing bankruptcy after more than a year without work. Both were deeply depressed, and with good reason. We thought of the man who had gone off his medication and was acting strangely, and of the woman who had checked herself out of rehab and clearly was drinking again. But we were in touch with these people. Whoever had written this cry for help was nowhere on our screen.

I now realized the enormity of our task. Even should the author have chanced into our midst, we wouldn't have been able to identify this person. Any of our parishioners could have written that letter. Shortly before my arrival as minister, a successful investment banker and leader of the congregation closed a lucrative deal one day and took his life the next. I myself remembered the boy with a perfect report card and perfect family who no longer could bear the weight of perfection. Attempting suicide, he, too, sought to end his secret pain. I should have known this lesson by heart.

For almost a decade, I remained in the dark about the author of this letter. Clearly he or she was depressed, perhaps even suicidal, but I could do nothing. I mentioned the letter in a sermon and later included it in my book *Lifelines*, partly in the hope that one or the other might prompt a visit. Still not a word. And then a miracle happened. I was leading the usual check-in that took place at the time before Wednesday-evening prayers in our chapel. During the service, everyone participated in Quaker fashion, praying in silence or out loud—as the spirit moved us. A sensitivity to what people were struggling with in their lives helped me open the service on the right note and also assisted them in preparing their hearts for worship.

"I have been wondering whether or not to tell you this," she said.

"What's that?" I asked.

"I'm anonymous," she replied.

"That's just fine," I said, not at all sure what she was getting at.

"I'm the anonymous parishioner who wrote you that letter, the one you put in your book."

This left me almost speechless. I scarcely knew this woman, not even by name until a month before, when she first joined our prayer circle. Had you asked me, all I could have told you about her is that her prayers were always prayers of thanksgiving. She spoke often of the joy she received from life and from our church. In eloquent, simple words, she mentioned little acts of kindness, given and received. "This is real wealth," she said once. "Kindness is life's true miracle. Love, life's greatest joy."

Experience teaches that, even as hell comes cloaked in many different guises, there are at least as many means to uncover heaven beneath them. An intensely private woman, she wouldn't accept my invitation to spell out to me how, but clearly she had found a means that worked for her. I'm sure it was hard. None of these ways is simple or painless. On earth, to get from hell to heaven, one must always pass through purgatory.

In the first chapter of the book of Genesis, God doesn't just proclaim "Let there be light, and there was light." It takes four days (in God's time) before the proper balance is struck between light and darkness. And still the darkness remains—in the firmament, between the waters, in our own lives. It is as if God keeps toying with the balance. Our lives are a little like that. We keep toying with the balance, also. The hope contained in these first few verses of the Bible is that, at the end of each, God says, "It is good."

The question remains, how can we distinguish the light of God, whether it be shining through the darkness or in the bright of day? As always, theology offers many different answers. To illustrate the varied ways in which God's presence might become apparent, consider three images drawn from optical technology: the magnifying glass, the prism, and the holograph.

With a magnifying glass, on a sunny day we can go outdoors, focus the otherwise imperceptible rays of the sun on some dry leaves, and they will catch fire. The rays of the sun beat down everywhere, of course, but lacking the focus offered by the glass they are not transformed into a tangible power that can ignite tinder into burning ash. According to this model, two things are required for God's power to evince itself. First, the human soul must be prepared. Even as wet leaves will not ignite in response to the sun's rays, an unreceptive soul would prove immune to the outpouring of God's grace. Second,

God's presence must be focused. In traditional Christian parlance, the magnifying glass that focuses God's presence upon a receptive soul is the gospel.

This metaphor offers a "hot" model of the way God might become manifest to the human soul. It also explains why God's presence is not universally felt across all of human experience. God is with us always, but lacking focus and our own receptivity, we lack evidence. On the other hand, those who experience God through the glass of the gospel are set afire by the Holy Spirit and transformed, even as dry leaves are ignited and transformed by the focusing of the sun's rays through a magnifying glass.

The prism offers a different, "cooler" model, by which God—still transcendent—might be experienced objectively. A prism catches the light and breaks it into its component parts. These, too, are evident only with the aid of an instrument, in this case not the gospel but the human mind, through which life's manifold appearances are filtered in search of some pattern to explain not only their complexity, but also their symmetry and orderliness. The cool model has long been a favorite among rationalists. During the Enlightenment, it led to the argument from design. Focused through the prism of thought, the spectrum of reality was perceived as so intricate and orderly as to demand the original efforts of a creative mind. If the hot view of God tends, in the West at least, toward a personal God who invokes a pietistic response in the hearts of his children, the cool view elicits a distant and respectful reverence for a much more impersonal divine master of ceremonies. By worshipping this God, many of my own Unitarian forebears legitimately earned the epithet (now shared with Episcopalians) of "God's frozen people."

The third optical image, one more promising to a twenty-first-century theology, is the holograph. Hot and cool, the holograph differs from the magnifying glass and prism even as they, each being theologically one-dimensional, resemble each other. The holograph offers a reflexive (both transcendent and immanent) image for God. It works in conjunction with a laser, which records images on a photo plate made up of thousands of tiny lenses. The result is a three-dimensional holograph, like those you have seen in the Haunted Mansion at

Disneyland or on your charge card. Mysteriously, if the photo plate is broken to bits and only a single shard of the original is employed for projection, the entire image, howsoever faint, will be replicated.

Our bodies, too, are holographic. Each of our cells contains the full genetic coding or DNA for our whole being, an equally telling metaphor for the reflexive nature of divinity. Even as each organism is a colony of cells and organs, each marked with the same DNA, might not everything that lives be said to create a larger organism marked with the DNA of God?

You may have noted that I exclude mirrors from this array of optical images. If you wish to refract God's light into meaning, don't look to mirrors, especially rearview mirrors. Rearview mirrors almost never work. We can learn lessons by looking back on our behavior with clear eyes, but almost never can we balance the light and darkness in our lives in the mirror of the past. Reflecting lost or stolen happiness, mirrored images are reminders of dreams we have let slip away or that others have dashed. Whether recollecting another's actions, our own misdeeds, or things otherwise fated (by our given parents, the color of our skin, our gender, sexual orientation, or the economic stratum into which we were born), such reflections may help us apportion blame, but they do little to lift life's burden.

To abandon our hopes to the future—how often we are consumed by worry about things that never happen—serves us no better. God's light shines only on the present. Only an ability to discern the light within each passing moment can redeem our days from the pain that abides within them.

In the Greek Orthodox Church, out of the cool darkness of an early spring evening, the celebration of Easter begins with the blessing of new fire. Struck from flint, this new fire passes from one candle to another until the church is filled with light. Trappist monk and modern mystic Thomas Merton describes how, long ago on Easter night, Russian peasants would carry the new fire home back to their cottages. "The light would scatter and travel in all directions through the darkness, and the desolation of the night would be pierced and dispelled as lamps came on in the windows of the farmhouses one by one." Emerging from the darkness out of deathly shadows, new fire is kindled from candle to candle, lighting home after home. "Even darkness, even evil, even death, seen by the light of the sacramental fire...can contribute accidentally, but existentially, to the life, growth and liberty of our souls," Merton observes. "And [in] the night then: the night of inertia, anguish and ignorance...is the passage through non-being into being, the recovery of existence from non-existence, the resurrection of life out of death."

To practice spreading light in the darkness does not mean extinguishing the darkness. This we cannot do. But we can—if free from the grip of fear—see that shadows are only the action of light being cast. By catching but a glimmer of the powering light, we can both feel and see strange beauty, emerging from our waking dream of death to appreciate life more fully. As our eyes grow accustomed, we discover that we can see in the dark.

For my once-anonymous parishioner, love led her home through the light-riddled darkness from a personal hell to the doorstep of heaven.

Perhaps this is all we can hope for here on earth: heaven and hell at once, stark in juxtaposition, inviting us to enter the flames, daring us to strike a balance, challenging us to overcome our fears by opening our hearts, by daring to risk the insecurity love offers. If so, all we can hope for is certainly hope enough.

CHAPTER 23

At Home in the Universe

When we are at home within ourselves, we are at home everywhere. Yet to be at home within myself, I found I needed God's company. When God dwells in my heart, I abide in God's presence. I live in an apartment of the creation furnished by the creator. However humble—and its occupant but animated dust—when I make my home there the whole universe is my dwelling place. God's dominion is my domicile.

Nineteenth-century transcendentalist Margaret Fuller once proclaimed, "I accept the universe." Fuller's contemporary, the Scottish essayist and philosopher Thomas Carlyle, responded acidly, "By gad, she'd better." He was thinking of the universe as housing for our bodies; Fuller celebrated it as her soul's true residence. When our soul is at home in the universe, the universe makes its home in our soul. In the strangest way, God and we are roommates. We may pay the bills, but God subsidizes the rent. We buy the food, but God makes it grow. Being human, at times we falter. But God grants forgiveness to a forgiving heart. And though fear and anger have their way with us at times, when tempered and redeemed by love, our lives now and then are really quite lovely.

"He walks with me and he talks with me," the old hymn sings of

Jesus. This is easier to imagine than walking and talking with God. By proclaiming Jesus fully God and fully man, ancient Christian theologians make intimacy with God a little more conceivable. My experience of God is personal also; not that God is a person but that I am. As a "personified" part of the creation, I best relate to that aspect of the creator that encompasses personality. The trinity works nicely for me this way: God above us, God within us, and God among us. Unitarian Universalism being a nondoctrinal faith, I am one universalist who finds the trinity, freely interpreted, more suggestive of God's possible nature than is undifferentiated oneness. This particular aspect of the old Christian mythos liberates my mind to explore the creation more creatively.

I am aware that myth makes people nervous. How eagerly it is abjured by biblical literalist and logical positivist alike. There is a fundamentalism of the left as well as of the right. If grounded in a radically different set of principles, the approach is similar. Positivists and fundamentalists share a penchant for thoroughgoing rationalism.

Take the Bible. Both true believer and hardcore atheist test it for its facts. To the former they are absolutely convincing. Following the logic of one fundamentalist leader—"I believe that Jonah was a literal man who was swallowed by a literal fish and vomited up on a literal beach"—the scriptural record is an exact transcript of events as they actually occurred. The skeptic finds this incredible and loses his or her faith. Both forget that the Bible is a religious storybook, not a historical record that will stand or fall only on its facts. It is a storybook rich with mythic overtones and parabolic undertones, helping us to set humanity in divine, and divinity in humane, perspective. As for its stories, like every story, their truth depends entirely upon their listeners. They will prove as true as love and hope are true, but only if they awaken us to possibilities for love and hope within our lives.

We are back in the fields surrounding Bethlehem. Suddenly, the sky shines with a great light, an angel of God. We are terrified, but the angel says, "Be not afraid; for behold, I bring you glad tidings of great joy, which will be to all people." What could be simpler or more startling? A child is born: the spark of cosmic consciousness planted in animal flesh; the miracle of human birth fixed at the cross point of the vertical axis, which is God's axis, and the horizontal axis, which is the axis of temporal as opposed to eternal things. Here birth, death, and eternity link inextricably in a mythic pattern expressed within a parable. As Emerson reminds us, "Infancy is the perpetual Messiah, which comes into the arms of fallen men and pleads with them to return to paradise." With every birth, something of eternity is made incarnate in time. In this sense, not only does Jesus's birth prefigure our own, but also, in the bloom of its promise, the birth of the baby Jesus witnesses to the limitless nature of our possibilities. Placed within our arms, Jesus reawakens us to the miracle of our own existence.

The creation itself inspires awe and beckons exploration. But the vastness of the universe also makes it difficult for us to feel at home there. In face of infinitude, we sense ourselves shrinking into infinitesimal insignificance. To strike up a personal relationship with the creator is inconceivable at times, especially the God of the scientists, caricatured by some as a "great oblong blur." As poet George Herbert observed, in contrast to the Bible (which for him lights the way to eternal bliss), "Stars are poor books, and oftentimes do miss." The philosopher Blaise Pascal, who kept abreast of the science of his day, reported from experience that one, "feeling himself suspended between the two abysses of nothingness and the infinite in this mass given to him by nature, will tremble." And yet I can't help but think of the words my father put on his tombstone.

Looking to the heavens when composing the words for his own grave marker, American poet Conrad Aiken spiced my father's humility with a dash of humor. As the story goes, on a visit to Savannah, Georgia, Aiken was struck by the name of a boat he saw in the harbor: *Cosmic Mariner.* Curious as to her itinerary, he consulted "The Shipping News," only to discover that the itinerary posted there said simply, "Destination unknown." Inspired by this serendipitous juxtaposition, he fashioned the following epigraph:

CONRAD AIKEN

COSMIC MARINER

DESTINATION UNKNOWN

In the true poetic spirit, Aiken is right. Our spiritual journey from birth to death is a cosmic pilgrimage as well as an earthly one. This requires a new religious model, its nature suggested by that memorable image of the blue-green earth twirling in space, rising over the moon's horizon.

Even as we can now view the earth from space, it is also becoming clear that we are spun from star stuff. That we are composed of the very matter that comprises our home invests our earthly journey with metaphysical moment. We move within and beyond ourselves into a new realm of encounter and discovery. Ancient cartographers would illustrate seas beyond the limit of the known world with monsters: "Here there be dragons." Yet travelers who venture to map the human soul can return through the gates of the unknown with a profound sense that—at the outer limits of their vision—they have caught within themselves a glimpse of God's inner sanctum. Another way to discover ourselves within the cosmos is to discern the cosmos within us.

Henry David Thoreau did precisely that, describing his own spiritual science as "home-cosmography." Seeking evidence of the divine within the ordinary and God's residence within his own mind, he traveled within himself on a cosmic mission.

> I hear beyond the range of sound,
> I see beyond the verge of sight,
> New earths—and skies—and seas—around,
> And in my day the sun doth pale his light.

Here Thoreau sounds very much like his teacher, Ralph Waldo Emerson. I still question Emerson's sovereign individualism, but theologically, he is among my favorite guides. To the cosmic voyager, Emerson cautions, "Thou seek'st in globe and galaxy, He hides in pure transparency." Rather than losing himself in the cosmos, Emerson perceives God's tracings in the most intimate created object. For Emerson, "the fresh rose...gives back the bending heavens in dew." He views his own life through the same cosmic microscope. Finding a fresh rhodora on one of his many walks through the woods neighboring Concord, a recognition of divine kinship tempers his solitude. Of this beauty ("its own excuse for being") Emerson ponders,

I never thought to ask, I never knew;
But, in my simple ignorance, suppose
The self-same Power that brought me there brought you.

One of Emerson's tough-minded critics, the philosopher George Santayana, dismissed the sentimentality of transcendentalism, while admiring Emerson's ability to entrance an audience. "They flocked to him and listened to his word, not so much for the sake of its absolute meaning as for the atmosphere of candor, purity, and serenity that hung about it, as about a sort of sacred music." With a tin ear for Emerson's brand of sacred music, Santayana truly puzzled over his appeal. The man had no doctrine. The deeper he got into something, the vaguer and more metaphorical Emerson became. "Did he know what he meant by Spirit or the 'Over-Soul'?" Santayana asks. "Could he say what he understood by the terms, so constantly on his lips, Nature, Law, God, Benefit, or Beauty? He could not."

Santayana is right. Mythic and parabolic language is imprecise. All Emerson could do was mirror his awe and humility in childlike reverence for the creation and his small yet consciousness-charged place in it. Santayana was at home in his books and nothing if not confident in his aesthetic doctrine; Emerson, like Margaret Fuller, was at home in the universe, because the universal God dwelled in his mind and heart.

Emerson would have understood Santayana's criticism, having cautioned, "Heaven walks among us ordinarily muffled in such triple or tenfold disguises that the wisest are deceived and no one suspects the days to be gods." He resisted codifying his experience of life and God into doctrine for another reason as well. He had no interest in others seeing through his eyes. For Emerson, a true disciple would be one who would greet each dawn in a new way, one unique to his or her particular insight and vision. For this same reason, he called on American artists and philosophers to liberate themselves from thralldom to the received Old World models—not that these were false or bad in and of themselves, only that what was authentic to the experience of others would prove inauthentic for a different time and place. Not only is derived experience certain to leave the creation muffled in multifold disguises, but there also are as many gates to perception as exist travelers who would venture to enter them. Since no doctrine can possibly encompass our collective intuition or experience of God, neither can one individual walk for another down the road that leads to God. Each of us defines the road we take and our heart determines its destination. This understanding, too, radiates from the hub of universalist theology. It connects us from the rim of our being to the center of all that is.

Whenever someone asks me, or I ask myself, "What have I done to deserve this?" the larger answer is always, "Nothing." We did nothing to deserve being born. We did nothing to earn life's privileges of joy and pain. And on the day we die, we will still know almost nothing about what life was all about. Life on this planet is billions of years old. Our span of three score years and ten (give or take a score or two) is barely time enough to get our minds wet.

By cosmologists' latest reckoning, there are some 100 billion stars in our galaxy, and ours is one of perhaps 100 billion galaxies. There are as many stars in the heavens as there are grains of sand on all the earth. And that is only our cosmos. There could be others. Divide the stars among us and, in our galaxy alone, every individual alive on earth today would be the proud possessor of some seventeen personal stars. If you choose to name yours (actually a fun thing to do), you can't start too soon. Naming one's own stars is more than a lifelong project. By my reckoning, the cosmic star-to-person ratio is 1.7 trillion to one.

So what do we do? Do we name our stars and shake our heads in humility and wonder? No. We sit on a single grain of sand on this vast cosmic beach and argue over who has the goods on God. Is it the atheist or the theist? The Hindu or the Buddhist? The Catholic or the Protestant? The Muslim or the Jew? We duel (sometimes to the death) over which religious teacher has the best insider information on God and the afterlife. Is it Jesus? The Buddha? Muhammad? How about Nietzsche, Gandhi, or Freud? Billions of accidents conspired to give each of these compelling teachers the opportunity even to teach. Knowing this—pondering numbers beyond reckoning—doesn't strip me of my faith. It inspires my faith. It makes me humble. It fills me with awe.

If our religion doesn't inspire in us a humble affection for one another and a profound sense of awe at the wonder of being, one of two things has happened. It has failed us, or we it. Should either be the case, we must go back to the beginning and start all over again. We must reboot our lives until the wonder we experience proves itself authentic by the quality of our response to it. The secret lies in how we treat one another. I may not believe as Jesus did, but I should dearly hope to love as Jesus did, to forgive and embrace others as unconditionally as he. The principal challenge of theology today is to provide symbols and metaphors that will bring us, in all our glorious diversity, into closer and more celebratory kinship with one another as sons and daughters of life and death.

BOOK V

Love after Death

CHAPTER 24

Love and Death

Since my cancer returned, I have conducted many press interviews. Each gives me the opportunity to discuss a topic most people would rather avoid. They also present me with the privilege of sharing the saving power of my universalist theology. Among the most thought-provoking interviews was conducted by Bob Abernethy of PBS, who excerpted segments of it for his news program Religion & Ethics NewsWeekly.

Q: There came a day in 2006 when you received a call from your physician. Tell me the story.

A: He called right after I'd had a barium esophagram and said, "Bad news. It looks like you have inoperable esophageal cancer." I asked him how long I had. He said, "Months, probably just a few. We'll try to make you comfortable." My wife was just taking off that very day for India, and my first major task was to make sure she kept her life going while I was helping to keep mine from falling apart. For about three weeks I thought I had three months to live. It soon became clear that they could operate. They did. And they operated quite successfully. I had more than a year's reprieve before the cancer returned in February of 2008 in an incurable form.

Q: What's your outlook now?
A: The treatment has been remarkably successful. I'm on an experimental treatment, being gifted a month at a time, and rejoicing in that. But eventually the treatment will lose its valance, and the barbarians will storm the gate and take the castle.

Q: How long do you think you have?
A: I've tried to stop guessing. I've predicted my demise too often and too early to continue to do so. So I will just accept whatever comes. If I were to guess, I would wager less than a year. This eventually will stop working, this treatment, and then the cancer—I've got cancer in my lungs and in my liver—will quickly spread. When it does, I will no longer be resistant to it. [As of May 2009, aided by the substitute treatment my oncologist, Dr. David Kelson, introduced when my first chemo regimen finally failed, the tumors are shrinking again.]

Q: You have written about your surprising acceptance of what has happened.
A: It was right after my wife went away for three days. I sat down with my closest friends and with Gary Dorrien of Union Theological Seminary to test this acceptance. I didn't bargain. I didn't get angry. I was surprised to go almost directly to acceptance. I skipped disbelief and anger and shock and resentment. And I tested that response because I was unsure of it, whether I was just hiding myself in a pink cloud. Every minister spends a lifetime preparing to ace the death test. We can't fail that test, having gone through it with so many others. It would cast a shadow back on our ministries if we were not able to embrace death and welcome it as an actual part of living, even as we have encouraged our parishioners to do. But I did discover something that I hadn't recognized before. I've always been amazed that some people, regardless of how physically ill they are, seem to go gentle into that good night and some seem to fight bitterly all the way. There's some courage in the fighting. I understand that. But there may be, in many cases, a fundamental difference between the embracers and the fighters. All of us die in the middle of our

story. There is a difference, however, between having ongoing business, which we all have, and having unfinished business. Each person knows what it is in his or her life. The one thing you've postponed doing, waiting for the right time. Or something you've done that you can't forgive yourself for. Whatever it happens to be, if you're given a terminal sentence, you may not have time to finish your unfinished business, and that casts a pall of regret over your life. Your final days are lived regretting what you have not done, or have not stopped doing in some cases, rather than freeing you to embrace the past, say yes to it, and then live fully in the present in a way that you were really never ever able to do before.

Q: That's what's happening to you now?
A: That's what's happening to me. It's a Buddhist notion, in many ways. I call it nostalgia for the present, looking forward to the present, not being caught up in things we can't do anything about. When you're living in the rush of life it's very difficult spiritually to focus on that present. When you are given a terminal illness and are not regretful of your past, you can embrace your life and say yes to it. Then you can live each day and fill it with all of its amplitude, all of its glory. You can celebrate what is, not mourn what is not.

*Q: You have a reference in your book [*Love & Death*] to those sad words, "if only."*
A: The two saddest words in the English language are "if only," and they ring with the most poignancy at a time when a person gets a word that he or she has a terminal illness. If only I had stopped drinking. If only I had dared to change careers when I could. If only I had reconciled with my father when I had a chance. Those "if only" questions which cannot easily or even practicably be answered in the last innings of one's life cast a pall over those days and lead to an enormous feeling of regret.

Q: Suppose you do have a lot of regrets, a lot of unfinished business. What then? What do you do?
A: Well, I have seen some amazing two-minute drills—people who

have, during their last days or weeks, somehow worked the wrinkles out, reconciled with their children, say, did the things that they needed to do to make peace with life, to make peace with God. The people who have pulled this off demonstrate spectacular acts of courage. The level of difficulty of the dive is high, however. You don't have much time. You must concentrate your whole life on redeeming that which is past, rather than moving gently forward into the next chapter. It's therefore good to take care of unfinished business before the last chapter of your life opens before you.

Q: When you've failed to do this, how then do you make up for it?
A: There are some things you cannot make up for. What you try to do is to jar yourself into the moment, to take your regrets and your expectation and try to let go of them. You may have blown things in the past, don't blow this. You still have time. In my case, when I was talking about not having unfinished business, my wife quickly pointed out to me, "Well, you may not have unfinished business, Forrest. But your children have unfinished business, and I have unfinished business, so let's get down to it." I realized this wasn't just my death. This was our death. That focused my attention in on them, on their needs, on our shared journey. All of a sudden life was filled with intrigue and wonder and challenge, but a different challenge than I had imagined. This is also one way to make up for past regret. Change the subject to the present. Redeem the day.

Q: When you received your diagnosis, what did you say to your children, and what did you invite them to say to you?
A: Well, each one is different. We have four children, and each child had a different set of issues. But the one thing I learned was that I couldn't make this right for them. One of my jobs in life, I've always felt, was to make things right, to make things work, to make people happy. I couldn't do that here. I had to listen to their pain, pain I had inadvertently caused. I had to let them express it. I still have to do that, although we've now, since I've had these dual six-month diagnoses, gotten pretty good at circling the wagons and lighting the campfires and crying together and then singing the old songs.

Q: A lot of crying?
A: There were a lot of misty eyes at first, often the crying ignited in me by them. Again, I didn't want my death to be a bother to people. That was simply a wrong call. I wanted everything to just go on as if nothing were happening. I wanted the house to be happy, but the house wasn't going to be happy. It's one thing for me to make my peace with God and leave. It's another thing for my children or my wife to be abandoned. That is where I had some growing left to do, in letting them call the shots, letting them let me know what they needed when they needed it and responding to their needs by listening more than by talking. I've always talked my way through and out of things. This was a time to listen, embrace, and say I'm sorry, when being sorry was an appropriate response. That helped bring them around to the point where now they are, I think, in a certain way, embracing my death as well, that is to say, learning from my dying, even as I hope they have learned from my life.

Q: You have expressed an idea about talking to your children as the end came.
A: As I've said before, the goal is to shut up and listen, to hear where they are coming from, what their needs are, not to try to make things that aren't right for them prematurely right. Let them express themselves. Let them work it through and embrace wherever they are, and then begin moving from there. It's not a one-evening proposition. And different ones of the children will respond in different ways. Some children will express their needs clearly. Others will have to have their needs sought out: "Tell me what you really feel." You need to be direct with them, more direct than I often am.

Q: You referred to the idea of getting permission to die. What does that mean?
A: People too often feel that they're failing their loved ones when they die. I can understand that. A father is abandoning his family, let's say, or a mother is abandoning her children. They feel that they have to hang on, that death is a defeat. So as long as everyone is telling them, "You can make it. Don't give up—you can beat this," if a lie surrounds

the proceedings, when the person is not making it and not beating it, she's going to feel that she's failed the very people who said, "You're going to make it"—her children, for instance. So her children have a loving obligation (and her spouse has a loving obligation) when the time comes to say, "It's okay. We're ready for you to go. We love you. We thank you for everything you've done. Godspeed you on your journey." In a way, giving death becomes like giving birth. It's "You're getting closer. You're going to make it. It's beautiful. You're doing great." That's what happened when my father-in-law died. My wife and her mother and sister were coaching him, holding his hand, urging him onward, telling him that everything was going to be okay, that he was almost there, that he was going to make it. By giving permission for our loved ones to die, they can die without their last thought being, "I am failing those who need me most."

Q: What has been the role of God in all this experience?
A: God is what sustains me. I am connected umbilically, I feel, with God's grace and power. It's not an omnipotent God. God didn't do this to me. God doesn't throw babies out of third-story windows or cause tsunamis. God is that which is greater than all and yet present in each. When that which is present in you relates to that which is present in all, you are sustained. You are billowed on the ocean of divinity and made safe. There's a great degree of safety in being a part of, rather than being apart from, the ground of your being.

Q: As a Unitarian Universalist, what was your idea of God in years past, and how did that evolve or change?
A: I began believing in a kind of rational God. It was an intellectual, head-trip God. I was closer to a Jeffersonian Unitarian than I was to an Emersonian Unitarian. Mine was a scientific entrée to divinity. I divided the rational from the irrational, missing the transrational realm entirely. Over time, partly through crises in my own life, very much through sitting by my parishioners at their bedsides and through my father's death, God moved from my head to my heart. As I've said many times, "God" is not God's name. "God" is our name for that which is greater than all and yet present in each.

It's our own construct. The word, "God," is a symbol. It's an arrow pointing toward a reality invested at the heart of our being.

Q: Is God, for you, a person?
A: I am a person, so I relate to the personal part of God's amplitude. God is so much more than a person, however. Otherwise, God becomes an idol.

Q: For traditional Christians, beliefs in the afterlife, eternal life with God, heaven—these are very, very important beliefs and give people close to death great comfort. What is it that gives you great comfort?
A: I do believe that I came from God and that I shall return to God. It's just that the Christian definitions of heaven I received when I was young today seem like punishment for good behavior. An eternity of anything is frightening. I see eternity instead as depth in time, not a length of time. I see us connecting spiritually within a zone that can take us deep or help us soar, a zone that is available to us every minute we live. I have no idea what happens after we die. It cannot be stranger than this. Being alive is too strange for words. So I won't be the least bit surprised if all of a sudden everything is topsy-turvy and I'm in a new world. But I can promise you it won't be the world that is predicted by the theological pundits. Too much organized religion is a life-denying exercise. We are asked to put this world down and this life down in order to live forever. That leads us away from love to God and neighbor. It leads us away from our ethical imperative, from expressing our ultimate concerns in ways that are redemptive in this world and in our larger neighborhood.

Q: In Love & Death *you referred to your late father and indicated you wished you had been able to reconcile with him?*
A: I did reconcile with my father shortly after college, in the early 1970s. When he ran for president in 1976, I took six months off from school and campaigned for him. We had made complete peace with each other by then. He died in 1984, so that wasn't the issue. The issue then was that he had wanted to die differently than he did. My father always said, "I hope to be walking down the road toying a

thought, be struck by a heart attack and die instantly." He especially feared the recurrence of cancer, which indeed returned to claim him. He had had cancer when he was twenty-five years old and given only three months to live. I was two months old then. Cancer's first visit enhanced his life as well. It made him live his life fully and richly, prodding him to achieve his highest goals as quickly as he could. My father still died young. He died at fifty-nine. When I was diagnosed with my own cancer at fifty-eight, I figured this is clearly the way my story, too, was meant to turn out.

My father was wrong in wishing for an instant death, however. I learned from that. The second time around he actually did have three months to live, but that proved time enough. It was a period of reconciliation. He lacked due confidence in his legacy. He believed that once you were out of office and out of power, you were instantly forgotten. Those three months gave all of us, family and admirers alike, the opportunity to celebrate my father and his mighty work. A terminal illness offers one gift that is not given to someone who is, as it were, struck down by lightning. We are given the opportunity to receive and return the gift of love. That's why these months, however few, can be the most precious months of one's life.

Q: You have made great use of these months. You have been very productive and you've put down on paper your deepest beliefs. Let's talk about some of those.

A: My book *Love & Death* allowed me to write a coda to my pastoral theology, to my lifelong belief that love and death interwoven are the heartstrings of religion. I have a mantra that I've come to live by over the past few years, and it's served me very well. It is "Want what you have; do what you can, be who you are."

Wanting what you have recognizes that we tend only to want things that we don't have. It's like we're looking out through a many-paneled window with all sorts of different projects etched in each segment, our vocational projects, parent and child and friend projects; our hobbies and our health are framed there too. But we never look through the glass that says "health" until it clouds over. Then we push our nose right up against it. All we can see is the darkness in the glass, and our whole world goes dark. If we back up from it and say, "I want friends who love me. I want a family who's helping me. I want the sun to come up, and I want the day to be beautiful," all these things can come true, all these prayers can be answered. By wanting what you have, finally you admit to yourself, "I wouldn't be appreciating all of these things with nearly the same gratitude, if this one pane had not gotten dark."

Doing what you can means doing all you can, no more and no less. It's not just mucking by, but it's not trying to do more than you can do, either, not stretching yourself out so far that you can't help but force a failure.

Finally, to be who you are, probably the hardest task of all, is not to fake your existence. Each of us is unique, with unique flaws and gifts. The world doesn't owe us a living; we owe the world a living, our very own.

Q: Back to the core beliefs you've identified and put down. You said the secret of it all is "it's not about me."

A: It's not about me. That's right. We tend to promenade in our own light. Not only that, when we get bathed in light we forget what a great shadow we might be casting. Self-consciousness and consciousness are opposites. To the extent that we're self-conscious, or self-absorbed, we cannot be conscious of the world around us, of God, of our neighbors. Jesus's two great commandments, to love God and love our neighbors as ourselves, are the hearthstone of my faith. I have got to get out of the way of my own light and be more aware of my shadow to fulfill these two commandments. Fortunately, for a minister it's a little bit easier not to get too caught up in yourself, at least not for long. Whenever we get too caught up in our own petty grievances, resentments, disappointments, or failures, the window flies open and death blows all the detritus off of our plate. We confront things that really matter. We are in the bosom of a family that is grieving and trying to come together and trying to make sense of what life and death are all about. At such times, our self-absorption, all those little preoccupations that are nagging at us, becomes an embarrassment. It just disappears from the plate.

Q: There's another sentence that you wrote: the greatest of all truths, you said, is that love never dies.

A: Yes, love never dies. I'm not certain about life after death. I know, however, that love is immortal, that every act of love we perform in this life extends like a little catena of pearls. It's carried on into one life and then passed on into another, so that centuries from now, not named with our name nor signed with our signature, but initiated by us and borne by our heirs, our love lives on. That's the work of religion. The work of religion is to make sure that the love we spread carries further than the division and hate. Conversely, the danger religion poses is that we may end up defining ourselves against others rather than uniting with and for others, leaving a very different legacy.

Q: Is that what you mean when you speak about love after death?

A: Yes. There's life after death as well. I just don't expect that it's a personalized life. We came from the cosmos. We return to the cosmos. But the miracle lies not in living forever, it springs from living in the first place. The odds against our being here in the first place are infinitesimal. You have to go back not just to the right egg and the right sperm of your parents. You have to go back all the way through history. None of our grandparents and great-grandparents died before puberty. If you go back to the eleventh or twelfth century, most of us have some 2.5 million ancestors, all of whom made it and connected at the right time. For those of us with a European heritage, none of our ancestors died before puberty in the Great Plague, whose mighty scythe cut down half the continent's children. Then go back beyond that to our prehuman ancestors and the urparamecium, and then back farther to the pinball of stars all the way to the big bang. We're kinetically and genetically connected to everything that preceded us. The universe was pregnant with us when it was born. The odds against this are staggering. And so we miss it entirely when we say, "What did I do to deserve this?" We didn't do anything to deserve being alive. Yet every life sentence is also a death sentence. A woman gives death when she gives birth. With life comes the certitude, the promise of death. We should embrace that necessary bequest with the same kind of reverence that we embrace and celebrate our birth.

Q: Tell me a little more about the relationship between love and death.
A: The opposite of love is not hate. It is fear. Fear is what armors our hearts. If our hearts are armored, they'll never be broken. We do not have to worry as much about grief and pain at a time of loss, either due to death or betrayal. We don't have to worry about those things, because we have armored our hearts. When you open your heart, you become vulnerable, which means susceptible to being wounded. Grief is, in this sense, a gift. There is a direct ratio between grief and love. The more we grieve, the more we loved. The more we care, the more we're hurt. In the home of a dying loved one, to open your heart can be extremely painful, because there's such a deep sense of pending loss. But on balance, the gain is so much greater than the loss. Over time, we celebrate the love we shared. Grief becomes an afterthought to the love. But love *is* grief's advance party. There's no question about that.

Q: There's an undertaker in Michigan I interviewed, Thomas Lynch. He's a poet too. He says grief is the tax we pay on loving people.
A: There you go. That's it. That's good. I have seen so many people get hurt in love and then try to protect themselves against it, but when they protect themselves against love, they protect themselves from the only thing that is worth living for.

Q: As you look ahead to your own death, is there anything about either death itself or the immediate time leading up to it that frightens you? Are you afraid?
A: I'm not afraid, because I'm living so much in the present. I'm not afraid of what's going to happen in the immediate weeks, say, before I die. I've seen, however, that it can be brutal, and I anticipate it being painful, and myself being disoriented. But I'm not going to waste time living through that in anticipation before it happens.

I do know, particularly from my experience with my father, that there is a tendency among some people to disappear into themselves as they go through the final passage. This disappearing act involves some pain for all of your loved ones, because you are cutting them off. Perhaps letting go of your ties so that you can leave this earth more freely is natural. But it's something I hope not to do. I hope instead to hold on tight to my loved ones, remembering that this is more painful for them than it is for me. When my death is over, I will be at peace wherever I am, whether in heaven or sleeping eternally in the earth. I will be at peace, whereas they will be in turmoil. I pray that I will be able to overcome my own instinct, perhaps, to let go of them prematurely. I pray that I will hold on to them long enough and well enough that they will recognize my presence and my love even as I'm dying.

Q: You mentioned praying. To whom do you pray, and how do you pray?
A: Every day I pray to God for what I have. I pray to God for my wife and children's love. I thank God for giving me my parents. I pray to God for the sun to come up. I pray to God for the tasks I have to do, even today when they're more limited. I pray to God for all those things that I might otherwise take for granted. Such prayers (lived more than spoken) are always answered. I don't pray for miracles. I don't pray for God to cure my incurable cancer. Instead, I receive and consecrate each day that I'm given as a gift. My prayers are prayers of consecration. And if I've done something wrong, which I do every day, I ask for forgiveness, in part so that I'm able to accept myself and get back to the program.

Q: When you pray to God, do you have a picture in your head?
A: I don't have a picture. I have a sense of peace. I'm praying to the deepest part of me and the deepest part of the cosmos. I'm connecting. I'm reaching out, getting outside of myself, getting as far out as possible. I don't anticipate that there is a little set of headphones up there taking my instructions down and passing them along to underlings in a cosmic bureaucracy to act on or against. My God doesn't work that way. Prayer or meditation (or simply reverent attention) connects us to the All. This connection is a healing connection. It

connects us to ourselves, giving us integrity, giving us peace of heart and mind. And it connects us to others, through forgiveness and reconciliation. I pray for people from who I'm estranged. I pray that they will have a good day. I picture their faces in my mind and remind myself that they're going to die, too. We're all mysteriously born and fated to die. Truly, we are one. These moments of oneness are moments of religious peace for me. Finally, I pray to be reconciled with or be one with God, both the creator and the cosmos. In each instance, the goal is to move from division to wholeness. When you're divided against yourself, estranged from your neighbor, or alienated from God, you live in a state of sin. Salvation comes in the eternal now, when you're at peace with yourself, can embrace your neighbor, and say yes to God.

Q: For you, what is the essence of Christianity?
A: I'm a Christian universalist. I believe that the same light shines through every religious window. The windows are different. The images cast through my Christian window and the others by the one light are therefore interpreted in different ways. Fundamentalists of the right say that the light shines through their window only. Fundamentalists of the left, looking at the bewildering variety of windows and worshippers, say that there is no light. But the windows aren't the light. The windows are where the light shines through.

Q: What do you do if you can't love?
A: If you can't love, you have probably been very badly hurt. There are some people who are pathologic in their indifference or hatred. There are some people who are born, evidently, without the empathy gene. I exclude them from my general analysis here. They certainly exclude me. But for most of us, love is an ongoing opportunity that can very easily be trampled on, sacrificed, from the very earliest days of one's life. Child abuse can take away your trust in life. Abandonment can take away your trust. So there are many reasons to harden one's heart. But however good a reason you may have, and I counsel with people who at the age of fifty-five and sixty are still agonizing over the damage their parents did to them, the only way to reconcile

yourself, to make peace with yourself, to make peace with your neighbor, to make peace with God and find salvation, is to break through and love, to forgive and to love. You don't change the person you forgive. You change your own heart. Once you have reconciled yourself to others and accepted yourself, at the end of your life, when you're given but a few months to live, you can look back without regret, you can look back in peace, and you can move forward with an embrace of each day that is given to you, the opportunities that it affords, and the opportunity it gives you to relate more profoundly with your family, your loved ones, and your God.

Q: That ability to live in the now is something you are experiencing greatly?
A: I have preached on living in the present for my entire career. In large measure, I was preaching to myself. I was hung up in the past and apprehensive about the future, mostly about things that never happened or ever would. But I knew that we could act only in the here and now. I knew that past and future were each a chimera. We make up the past sifting selectively and creatively through our experiences, and the future is a complete crapshoot. Only in the here and now can we love God, love our neighbor, and redeem the day. That is one of the truly beautiful things about a terminal illness. Yes, there's a lot of pain, discomfort, and agony that goes with it, but if you have made peace with your past and have no unfinished business, you are invited into the present. Your friendships become stronger. Your love becomes more vital. Every day becomes more beautiful, a gift unto itself. All you have to do is unwrap it. You unwrap the present and receive it as the gift it is. That simple act is, for me, anyway, an unexpected boon during this time of trial. I walk through the valley of the shadow, and it's riddled with light.

CHAPTER 25

Love's Tribunal

As I stroll through the valley of the shadow of death, I continue to live, in some ways more abundantly. I also continue to tweak and sharpen my theology. Galen Guengerich, my successor as the senior minister of All Souls, graciously cedes his pulpit to me once a month. I close this section of final thoughts with an excerpt from my sermon of February 15, 2009, which further develops my ideas on love, death, and universalism (which is love's gospel).

We can arrange the pictures on the walls of our mind in any way we choose. As I slowly die of terminal cancer, blessed with the opportunity to rearrange those pictures more thoughtfully, I fill my memory wall with images of love. The pictures that adorn my mind illuminate my life. Past and future disappear. In time's eternal depth, through love's portals we enter heaven on earth. One with God, self, and neighbor, we are saved.

As I reflect on this life lesson, it grows in both clarity and power. I know how deeply love can hurt and how sensible it may seem sometimes to rip its recurring promise from the tapestries of our lives. I also know how tempting it can be to cloak our hearts to protect them not only from the pain of betrayal but also from the abiding pain of loss.

The courage to die is nothing when compared to the courage of those who live on after us, their hearts bereft by loss. Yet it is precisely at these moments when we are invited to stand before love's tribunal to be judged. Are you guilty of love or not guilty? That is life's ultimate question. Again and again over the course of a lifetime we are brought before the tribunal of love, where those innocent of love are damned and the guilty are saved.

In its Latin root, "salvation" means health, in the same sense that the Teutonic words "hale," "whole," and "holy" are cognates. Sin, in contrast, speaks of disease: of division, brokenness, and estrangement. This is the human condition. We live our lives, to one extent or another, in a state of sin. Haunted by our conscience, which is one instrument of judgment at love's tribunal, we are often at odds with our better selves.

We also live divided from our neighbors, from our enemies, even from our loved ones, those nearest and most dear. In fact, who knows better how to hurt our loved ones than we do? Over time, we may grow so expert at this that no one, their worst enemy included, could administer an equal shot of pain.

Finally, we live estranged from God, from the ground of our being. Taking life for granted rather than receiving it as a gift, sometimes even actively begrudging it, we ask of life the most impertinent question of all: What did I do to deserve this?

As categorized by the ancient Greeks, there are three types of love: *eros; philia;* and *agape.* Eros, the form of love most easily twisted, is romantic in nature. We may fall in love and keep on falling until we hit the rocks; or we may fall in love to be caught and cradled in another's arms. Here is eros's secret: Only the love we give away can save us, not the love we grab and squeeze so tightly against our breast that we crush it. Only when it focuses our hearts on the needs and desires of our loved one, not on our own needs and desires, can eros save.

Philia, the second type of love, is friendship: brotherly and sisterly love. Friendship is the archetype for human affection. Emotionally less complicated and demanding than eros, philia unites us in the saving bonds of community. We are a part of, not apart from, our neighbors, whom we love as ourselves. That is to say, if eros is "Love Me Tender," philia is "Stand By Me." Philia is not reserved for our friends alone. It spills over into our families as well. For example, though eros plays its initiating role, ultimately it is philia, not eros, that forms the foundation for a good marriage.

The third type of love, agape, is God's love. It gives freely and continuously, demanding nothing in return save that we open our hearts and minds to its grace. In human experience, agape is kindness. Without need or expectation of any quid pro quo, we simply give love away. More universal than philia and exponentially more inclusive than eros, agape can be as simple as a large tip or as sweet as a gentle word to someone we will likely never see again. Agape doesn't leave its heart in San Francisco; it takes its heart with it wherever it goes, lightening the world's burdens one tiny grace note at a time. As administered by the human heart, God's love is life's most unselfish gift.

If there are three types of love, there are also three contexts in which love does its healing work. To explore each of these, I invite you to stand before love's tribunal. Here you must answer three simple questions. Do you love yourself? Do you love your neighbor as yourself? And do you love God, or whatever you may choose to call that which is greater than all and yet present in each, the life force, the holy?

First, have you made peace with yourself? Is your conscience clear? The theological word "atonement" means at-one-ment. Are you divided or at one? Have you reached the peace of acceptance? In short, do you love yourself?

Second, are you at peace with your neighbor? Are you reconciled with your loved ones, even with your enemies? Remember, we are more alike than we differ, yet it is the differences, so slight when viewed in the light of eternity, that estrange us from our blood brothers and sisters, from our honest to God, hope to die, kin. Have your achieved the peace of forgiveness? In short, do you love your neighbor as yourself?

Third, and finally, have you made your peace with God, with the mystery of creation, the ground of your being, with your life? Do you open your heart daily and with deep gratitude for the gift of life, undeserved, mysterious, abundant, challenging, difficult, and blessed? Have you attained the peace of consecration? In short, do you love your God?

Such moments of full health, wholeness, and holiness are rare indeed. Yet, if but once over the course of a lifetime, you find yourself presented at love's tribunal and can answer yes to each of these three questions, your life is redeemed, suffused with meaning and charged with purpose. Having made peace with life, you can make peace with death. By submitting to love's tribunal and answering yes to love's questions, you will know that your life has proved worth dying for.

Where Did We Come From?
Where Are We Going?

I close The Cathedral of the World *with a brief excerpt from my first book,* Father and Son: A Personal Biography of Senator Frank Church of Idaho, *written in the summer of 1984, three months after his death. My father's dying was a lesson in living. I pray that my own may be the same. As I lie dying, I trust that, having made peace with life, I can make peace with death. The heart of universalism is love, but its ultimate promise is peace.*

Two weeks after my father died, I had a new-member appointment with an engaging woman about my age, exactly half the proverbial threescore and ten. Her daughter and mine had just turned three. They were classmates during the week and at the church school on Sundays. We first met when she and her husband called on me to christen their daughter.

Near the end of our discussion, she asked me a question that I had a hard time answering. One of the reasons it was such a difficult question is that it came from her daughter. Children often ask better, harder, more important questions than we adults do. It is not their fault. They don't know any better.

In any event, this little girl asked her mother to tell her where she had been before she started growing in her mommy's tummy. I hasten to add that this little girl's mother did the sensible thing. She punted in hope for better field position on a later set of downs. She sat her daughter down and said, "That is a very good and very hard question, honey. I will think about it carefully, and then come back with an answer a little later." What she then did was a very rational, if unreasonable, thing to do. She went to her library, took out a book called *The Magic Years*, and started searching for clues.

Our children have a great, if unwarranted, sense of confidence in us, and this little story continues to demonstrate both sides of that equation.

"What are you doing, Mommy?"

"I am looking for the answer to your very good, very hard question," her mother replied.

If you do not have this book in your library, and are interested in the answer to this question, I can tell you that you will not find it there or in any book. For the little girl, however, the book became very important. Later that evening her father found her reading it upside down in the bathroom.

"What are you doing, sweetheart?"

"Mommy told me that I can find out where I was before I was born by looking in this book. But, Daddy," she said, "there aren't any pictures." At which point, as if I didn't have enough impertinent children of my own, this little girl's parents resolved to come to me in search of an acceptable answer.

Two days later, I was visiting one of our longtime members, a gentle, lovely woman, who had been a member of All Souls for almost fifty years and was in the hospital. We had a wonderful conversation. She was in good spirits and, given how much trouble she had been having lately, looked hale and beautiful to me. After our conversation had gone along for a while, she asked me, "Forrest, what do you think happens to us after we die?"

At that very moment it struck me. Not the answer, exactly. I really don't know the answer to that question. What struck me was that the two questions, hers and that of the little girl, were very much the same. "Where were we before we were born?" and "What happens to us after we die?" One is an important, existential question for the very young; the other an important, existential question for those of us who are nearing the end of our lives. I thought about my own age at the time, almost exactly halfway between that of this bright little girl and this strong and wise older woman. Weighing the questions one against the other, I felt deep within a balance point between them. Where am I? Am I halfway between nothing and nothing? Or something and something? Or everything and everything?

Of all that we experience, there is nothing more natural than birth and death. Nothing that happens between can even begin to approximate either birth or death in terms of absolute unadulterated naturalness. Birth and death are spontaneous acts, not conscious ones. They are perfect acts of nature. We know this about birth, I think, but death is somewhat different. One of the reasons that death is different from birth is that we are conscious of it in advance and are frightened by it.

Looking at this in a purely biological way, without death there would be no birth, not as we know it, for the simplest forms of life never die. For all practical purposes, single-celled organisms are immortal. In other words, we were immortal until we became interesting! On the one hand, this invites us to reconsider the advantages of immortality. Because we die, we are privileged to have been born. On the other hand, far from persuading us to disbelieve in immortality, this same observation challenges us to think about immortality in new, more dynamic, less selfish terms.

Let me take this one step further. For me it is a sufficient step. It is one of the reasons that I don't worry all that much about where I was before I was born and where I will be after I die. It is not that these are unimportant questions. It is just that for me the miracle lies in between. No experience of being, unknown to us and probably unknowable, that has taken place before this life or will take place after it, could possibly be more remarkable, more wonderful, or stranger than this life we share today. Life is a miracle couched between mysteries. It is a miracle incarnate, not a given, but a gift, an unaccountable gift. When we take it for granted, or beg for something more, we do it violence.

Nonetheless, these questions remain and they are not unimportant ones. So let me hazard an answer to each. My guess—and it is no more than a guess—is this. Before we are born and after we die, we are with God. We come from God, spend a lifetime imperfectly manifesting the promise of God incarnate as God-carriers, and then return to God when we die.

Admittedly, I have an unorthodox view of God, one I cannot prove. Nor would I even wish to try. For me, God is the genius of the life force, that which is greater than all and yet present in each. Try as I will, I simply cannot explain or understand the miracle of life, and, yes, of birth and death, in any other way. "God" is our name for the spirit that animates and impels and finally enfolds our lives into its own.

I don't anticipate that I, as a distinct individual, will be any more conscious of God, or of my participation in God, after I die than I was before I was born. All I know is that the miracle we participate in daily, this miracle of breathing, and thinking, and acting, and failing, and loving, and dying, is not wholly haphazard. Neither is it discrete, bounded by a distinct and absolute beginning and ending. We are a part of something larger, something ongoing and eternal, inscrutable perhaps even unto itself. Reflecting on the light that shines through my religious window, the more I contemplate this mystery the more reverent I become, the more undemanding of final answers, the more accepting of all that is, of all that was, and of all that will be.

Acknowledgments

In addition to Helene Atwan at Beacon Press, who has showed me only kindness during her years as publisher and editor in chief, I wish also to thank my superb editor, Amy Caldwell, for her enthusiasm and for helping me tighten the seams of my argument; Alex Kapitan for her careful reading of the manuscript and insightful suggestions; my attentive copyeditor, Melissa Dobson; Pam MacColl for her help with publicity; Sarah Laxton and Susan Lumenello for keeping me in the loop all the way; and associate publisher Tom Hallock for listening with his heart as well as his mind. As usual, my friend and literary agent, Wendy Strothman, performed her magic, for which, as always, I am deeply grateful.

I also owe a deep debt of gratitude to my many friends in ministry, foremost among them, from my own denomination, John Wolf, Galen Guengerich, Bill Schulz, Kay Montgomery, and Stephen Kendrick; Methodist minister Stephan Bauman; Presbyterian pastor Bill Grimbol; Disciples of Christ minister Bob Hill; and American Baptist minister Peter Gomes. My congregation, the Unitarian Church of All Souls in New York City, has offered the richest possible ground for the healthy growth of a contemporary universalist theology. And my historical guides over the years, from George Huntston Williams at Harvard to Gary Dorrien at Union, have given me a generous and learned context for my theology's development.

Abundant thanks to my dear friends, Robert Oxnam, Jack Watson, Peter Fenn, and Patrick Shea, seekers all, who read the manuscript and shared their thoughts, bolstering my confidence while guiding me with their companionable critique.

Finally, I thank my family, beginning and ending with my wife, Carolyn. Love is the beating heart of universalism. More than anyone, Carolyn, you have taught me the meaning of love.

Forrest Church

May 2009

Credits

Invocation: Adapted from *A Chosen Faith: An Introduction to Unitarian Universalism*, by Forrest Church with John A. Buehrens (Boston: Beacon Press, 1989).

Chapter 1: Adapted from *God and Other Famous Liberals: Recapturing Bible, Flag, and Family from the Far Right*, by Forrest Church (New York: Simon and Schuster, 1990).

Chapter 2: Adapted from *God and Other Famous Liberals*.

Chapter 3: Adapted from "The Role of Religion in American Democracy," published on the Web site of the Unitarian Universalist Association of Congregations, uua.org (fall 2007). Reprinted by Time.com (fall 2007).

Chapter 4: Adapted from "The American Creed," address delivered at Bangor Theological Seminary, Bangor, Maine, January 29, 2002.

Chapter 5: Adapted from "What Would Jefferson and Adams Do?" published online at uuworld.org (July 2006) by *UU World*, the magazine of the Unitarian Universalist Association of Congregations.

Chapter 6: Adapted from *The American Creed* by Forrest Church

Chapter 7: Adapted from *Spiritual Perspectives on America's Role as Superpower*, eds. editors at Skylight Paths (Woodstock, VT: Skylight Paths Publishing, 2003).

Chapter 8: Previously unpublished. Sermon preached at All Souls Unitarian Church, New York City, February 23, 2003.

Chapter 9: Adapted from "Chariots of Fire," keynote address for the tenth annual Interfaith Service for Peace, delivered at the Princeton University Chapel, Princeton, New Jersey, September 27, 1987. Reprinted in *Representative American Speeches* 1987–1988, ed. Owen Peterson (New York: H. W. Wilson, 1988).

Chapter 10: Adapted from "Fear and Terror," sermon preached at All Souls Unitarian Church, New York City, April 23, 1995. Reprinted in *Representative American Speeches* 1994–1995, ed. Owen Peterson (New York: H. W. Wilson, 1995).

Chapter 11: Adapted from "Shall We Overcome?" sermon preached at All Souls Unitarian Church, New York City, January 17, 1993. Reprinted in *Representative American Speeches* 1993–1994, ed. Owen Peterson (New York: H. W. Wilson, 1994).

Chapter 12: Adapted from "World Peace," sermon preached at All Souls Unitarian Church, New York City, January 3, 2000. Reprinted in *Yes to Peace: Sermons on the Shalom of God*, ed. R. Scott Colglazier (Atlanta: Chalice Press, 2001).

Chapter 13: Adapted from "Choose Life," sermon preached at All Souls Unitarian Church, New York City, Easter Sunday 2005. Reprinted by Beliefnet.com. Reprinted with permission from Beliefnet.

Chapter 14: Adapted from "Choose Your Enemies Carefully," sermon preached at All Souls Unitarian Church, New York City, May 16, 2006. Reprinted by uua.org.

Chapter 15: Adapted from "Religion and the Body Politic," sermon preached at All Souls Unitarian Church, New York City, October 27, 2008. Reprinted by Beliefnet.com and uua.org. Reprinted with permission from Beliefnet.

Chapter 16: Adapted from *The Search for Meaning: Americans Talk*

About What They Believe and Why, ed. Phillip Berman (New York: Random House, 1990).

Chapter 17: Adapted from "Universalism Yesterday and Today," keynote address delivered at the 151st Annual Session of the New York State Convention of Universalists, New York City, October 13, 1979. Reprinted in *The Universalist Heritage: Keynote Addresses on Universalist History, Ethics and Theology (1976–1991)*, ed. Harold H. Burkart (New York: New York State Convention of Universalists, 1991).

Chapter 18: Adapted from "Universalism in the Twenty-first Century," *UU World* (November/December 2001).

Chapter 19: Adapted from "Emerson's Shadow," *UU World* (May/June 2003).

Chapter 20: Adapted from "There Is No Hell," Beliefnet.com (2006). Reprinted with permission of Beliefnet.

Chapter 21: Distilled from *The Seven Deadly Virtues: A Guide to Purgatory for Atheists and True Believers*, by Forrest Church (New York: Harper & Row, 1989).

Chapter 22: Adapted from *Bringing God Home: A Spiritual Guidebook for the Journey of Your Life*, by Forrest Church (New York: St. Martin's Press, 2002).

Chapter 23: Adapted from *Bringing God Home*.

Chapter 24: Adapted from an interview on PBS's *Religion & Ethics NewsWeekly*, with host Bob Abernethy, broadcast October 2008. Reprinted with permission of *Religion & Ethics NewsWeekly*, a PBS production of Thirteen/WNET New York. All rights reserved.

Chapter 25: Adapted from "Love's Tribunal," sermon preached at All Souls Church, New York City, February 15, 2009; reprinted on Beacon Broadside (www.beaconbroadside.com), the Beacon Press blog.

Benediction: Adapted from *Father and Son: A Personal Biography of Senator Frank Church of Idaho by His Son*, by Forrest Church (New York: Harper & Row, 1985). Copyright © 1985 by F. Forrester Church. Reprinted by permission of HarperCollins Publishers.